The Euro 2020 B

Shane Stay

THE
EURO 2020
BOOK

Everything You Need to Know
About the Championship

Meyer & Meyer Sport

British Library Cataloguing in Publication Data
A catalogue record for this book is available from the British Library

The Euro 2020 Book
Maidenhead: Meyer & Meyer Sport (UK) Ltd., 2020
ISBN: 978-1-78255-200-0

© 2020 by Meyer & Meyer Sport (UK) Ltd.
Aachen, Auckland, Beirut, Dubai, Hägendorf, Hong Kong, Indianapolis, Cairo, Cape
Town, Manila, Maidenhead, New Delhi, Singapore, Sydney, Tehran, Vienna

Member of the World Sports Publishers' Association (WSPA), www.w-s-p-a.org
Printed by Books International
ISBN: 978-1-78255-200-0
Email: info@m-m-sports.com
www.thesportspublisher.com

CONTENTS

INTRODUCTION

The UEFA European Championship 2020.

First of all, for those of you wondering about the name: Yes, it has changed over the years. It was initially known as the European Nations' Cup (during 1960 and 1964), but from then on it became the UEFA European Football Championship, UEFA European Championship, or *simply* the UEFA Euro.

However, as many of you know, it is most commonly referred to as the Euro Cup, or simply the Euro, as in "Euro 2020." So don't be surprised to see a few different references regarding the Euro.

The premise is simple: Europe's best soccer-playing nations battle it out for the title. It is essentially like the World Cup of Europe and is in fact thought to be *the* tournament in Europe. Although it might initially sound like a paradox, many people think that the Euro is more competitive than the actual World Cup, and while this may be true, there must be a reason for people to think such a thing.

While the world's best soccer-playing talent is based in Europe, the World Cup limits the amount of teams that are able to qualify each year. Therefore, some of the best European teams are unable to compete, and these slots are instead given to the lesser-talented soccer-playing nations from North America, Asia, and Africa. An interesting argument arises: The teams from Europe that don't qualify for the World Cup would likely defeat most teams from North America, Asia, and Africa. So, therefore, the Euro Cup is the most elite tournament.

Some people might say, "But what about the South American Cup?" First of all, the name has changed to the Copa America. Secondly, South America realistically has four teams that are fighting it out for the title: Brazil, Argentina, Chile, and Uruguay. Despite Uruguay having had success in that tournament over the years, most people think that the real competition is between Brazil and Argentina, which is essentially true. Depending on the generation of players, Chile is another viable candidate (one that has been exceedingly good recently), while Colombia might also throw its hat into the ring from time to time. While this is quite rare, the rarer thing would be Ecuador and Venezuela making a case for the title. As for Peru, Bolivia, and Paraguay—we can forget about it. To be fair, in South America, it comes down to Brazil, Argentina, Chile, and Uruguay, and maybe, I stress *maybe*, Colombia. So, essentially, that's four teams. But let's just take a step back here. It should be known that for a "classic South American tournament," the 2019 Copa America included Qatar and Japan. Oy vey. That is very strange, there's no other way around it. They were included as 'invited' teams.* First of all, assuming the role of an odds maker, there is no way for Qatar to win that tournament. However, theoretically, there could be a chance that Japan—a very good soccer-playing nation—could walk away with the first-place trophy. But again, this would be very strange. Imagine that: "The winner of the 2019 Copa America—the elite tournament of South America—is…Japan."

---

* Geographically, the idea of Qatar and Japan being invited to the Copa America is rather insane. Whereas, in terms of geography, there have been extended discussions as to whether or not places like Israel and Turkey should be considered for European or Asian competitions, which is another story altogether, one that makes more sense than Qatar and Japan competing in the Copa America.

Putting everything aside, it really is just four teams competing for the Copa America.

Now let's look at Europe, shall we? The UEFA Euro has an intense field of competition. There's Germany, Spain, France, Netherlands, Italy, Russia, Portugal, Greece, Denmark, England, Sweden, Switzerland, Poland, Croatia, and many others. It is an amazingly talented field. When you take a step back, you realize why many people consider it on par with, or perhaps better than, the World Cup. This isn't to say that North America, Asia, and Africa have nothing to offer. Each continent is rising in the world of soccer, and it is very possible, though somewhat unlikely, for those participants to step ahead of Europe. As it stands, Europe is the center of the soccer-playing universe and that is not set to change anytime soon. The UEFA Euro stands alone as the leader of continental competitions, with the Copa America in South America having accepted second place. Although quality of play is already improving in North America, Asia, and Africa, Europe still holds all the cards. When it comes to the UEFA Euro, all eyes gravitate toward it. After all, outside of the World Cup, it is definitely the place to be.

STAY'S FAB 5: THE TOP 5 PLAYERS OF UEFA EURO 2020

Luka Modrić
Mbappé
Cristiano Ronaldo
Harry Kane
Eden Hazard

Plus 6:
Timo Werner
Jorginho
Julian Brandt
Marco Reus
Sergio Ramos
Thibaut Courtois

STAY'S UEFA EURO 2020 ALL-STAR 11 LINEUP

Who says we need "defenders" in the traditional sense? With a little work, these offensive powerhouses can transition into defensive roles that would unleash outright offensive magic. The 4-3-3 seems like the best formation for such a group. The possession would be off the chart, and few teams would be able to break through this organized defense.

Timo Werner   **Harry Kane**   **Cristiano Ronaldo**

Mbappé   **Luka Modrić**   **Marco Reus**

Julian Brandt   **Sergio Ramos**   **Jorginho**   **Eden Hazard**

Thibaut Courtois

Other players who deserve to be on this list:
Antoine Griezmann, Isco, Sergio Busquets, Ivan Rakitić, Ivan Perišić, Dele Alli, Harry Maguire, Memphis Depay, Frenkie de Jong, Matthijs de Ligt, Bernardo Silva, Toni Kroos, Serge Gnabry, Paulus Arajuuri, Birkir Bjarnason, Leonardo Bonucci, Marco Verratti, and too many others!

STAY'S BLAST FROM THE PAST SUPER TEAM

Now this was very tricky. How can you pick a starting 11 from all past Euros? It's impossible. You're inevitably going to leave someone out, well, multiple people in fact. There were so many players to consider but I had to do it. I had to come up with 11. But, I made a simple stipulation. Members of this blast from the past super team had to be part of a Euro championship team. Each player was evaluated based on how they performed in both Euro tournament matches and club competitions. After all, players are chosen for national teams based on how they perform at the club level. Here they are:

Marco van Basten   **Gerd Müller**   **Cristiano Ronaldo**

Platini

Zidane   **Xavi**

Paul Breitner **Franz Beckenbauer** **Frank Rijkaard** **Sergio Ramos**

Dino Zoff

There are so many other players that come to mind, ones that theoretically could and should be in this lineup, such as Karl-Heinz Rummenigge, Giresse, Tigana, Ruud Gullit, Ronald Koeman, Henry, Iniesta, and, well, maybe just everyone from Spain's 2008 and 2012 championships. How can you go wrong there? You can't, that's the thing.

As far as this lineup is concerned, there is not much to say. However, one position that was difficult for me was Gerd Müller's. This was only because I immediately thought about choosing David Villa or Henry instead for chemistry's sake. Gerd Müller is a great one, but in the flow of the game, I might prefer the gamesmanship and on-the-ball savviness of Villa or Henry. Having said that, how can you go wrong with Gerd? The answer is: You can't. He was a great finisher with an uncanny ability to put the ball in the back of the net. Furthermore, considering Henry's multi-talented ability, he could very well be one of the starting midfielders. During his time with Arsenal, he took over the field and really showed what he could do with the ball. However, there are plenty of other midfielders to choose from, some of which were mentioned (Iniesta in particular). Gullit, in all his brilliance, could theoretically have any team built around him and things would still fall in line. Lastly, as far as goalies go, you can take your pick. We could go back to Lev Yashin (the Soviet keeper for the 1960 championship side). There is also Harald Schumacher of West Germany. Then you have Iker Casillas from Spain, along with many others. But, really, how can you not have Dino Zoff? The great Dino Zoff. There's something about an Italian goalie—it just seems right.

Generally speaking, these players were very hard to select. Let's put it this way: Imagine if Dino Zoff, Walter Zenga, and Gianluigi Buffon were all the same age and they all showed up to the same tryout. How would you choose? It's unfair that two of those players would end up sitting on the bench. And that's the essence of a list like this.

When it's all said and done, it's a tough list to compile because there are so many options and combinations. It is almost unfair to suggest such a list in the first place. However, one had to be compiled and this one is very good. It is a great starting 11, one that has the capacity to astound any audience at any time. And, should any team ever face this group...I truly pity them.

This leads to the next team. Considering there are so many quality players to choose from, I had to put together a Blast from the Past B Team.

STAY'S BLAST FROM THE PAST B TEAM

David Villa   Karl-Heinz Rummenigge

Iniesta   Henry

Ruud Gullit

Nani   Marcel Desailly   Puyol   Tigana

Ronald Koeman

Iker Casillas

I know what you're thinking. Why would Nani be a defender? Here's the thing: Attacking players like Nani make great defenders. For starters, he knows all the dribbling moves so there is no chance of fooling him. Secondly, he is quick and fast like nobody's business. Lastly, he'd make a great attacking threat down the wing. If he didn't work out, we would bench him. Get over it. Same goes for Tigana. He was more of a midfielder, but, given his talent level, how can you resist having him on the team? Look, we could have gone back to 1968—when defenders stood around like cones—and chosen an Italian player. A safe steady Italian, the kind that played for Inter Milan for 5 million years. The kind that drank espressos at the nearby coffee bar with locals every morning before practice. Maybe Giacinto Facchetti. Instead, I chose to go off the grid and take a chance with Nani and Tigana. So there we have our B Team, and what a team it is.

You have Desailly and Puyol in the middle as all-out defensive stoppers. Behind them, backing with brilliant technical passing, is the one-and-only Ronald Koeman. Henry and Iniesta would work off of the brilliance of Ruud Gullit, and up top you have David Villa and Karl-Heinz Rummenigge acting as brilliant set-up players, giving Iniesta, Henry, Nani, and Tigana a vast amount of opportunities to work with.

This might be the "B Team" but realistically, it's an "A Team" in every sense of the word.

Now it is time to enter the amazing 2020 UEFA Euro tournament. When it's all said and done, 2020 is shaping up to be an amazing, historic year for European soccer. There is a talented field of teams with a number of frontrunners, which means that it is going to be an exciting tournament.

UEFA EURO 2020 QUALIFYING GROUPS

On route to UEFA Euro 2020, the teams had to battle it out in qualifying. Here's how the UEFA Euro 2020 Qualifying Groups looked:

Group A
England
Czech Republic
Kosovo
Bulgaria
Montenegro

England finished strong in first place. Czech Republic had a respectable second-place finish. This time around, it just wasn't happening for Montenegro.

Group B
Ukraine
Portugal
Serbia
Luxembourg
Lithuania

Ukraine surprised a few people by finishing in first, with Portugal in second. As for Lithuania, it just wasn't meant to be. In fact, Lithuania might want to reverse engineer what Ukraine was doing.

Group C
Germany
Netherlands
Northern Ireland
Belarus
Estonia

Germany and the Netherlands came out on top. No surprise there.
Estonia, well, what can you say?

Group D
Switzerland
Denmark
Ireland
Georgia
Gibraltar

The Swiss came out on top. You don't hear that too often. As for
Gibraltar, yeah, that's about right.

Group E
Croatia
Wales
Slovakia
Hungary
Azerbaijan

Croatia and Wales ended up leading the group. As for
Azerbaijan, it's back to the drawing board.

Group F
Spain
Sweden
Norway
Romania
Faroe Islands
Malta

Spain finished in first which surprised absolutely no one. Nor was anyone terribly alarmed that Malta and the Faroe Islands were battling it out for last place.

Group G
Poland
Austria
North Macedonia
Slovenia
Israel
Latvia

Poland did well to finish first. Latvia, on the other hand, has some work to do for next time around.

Group H
France
Turkey
Iceland
Albania
Andorra
Moldova

France and Turkey finished on top while Andorra and Moldova will have to regroup for the next Euro.

Group I
Belgium
Russia
Scotland
Cyprus
Kazakhstan
San Marino

Belgium was the clear winner in this group. San Marino—which had zero wins and 10 losses—didn't have a chance.

Group J
Italy
Finland
Greece
Bosnia and Herzegovina
Armenia
Lichtenstein

Italy finished well ahead of the pack. Liechtenstein didn't exactly have anything to write home about, unless you consider "losses" an interesting letter. Liechtenstein won zero games, though, in its defense, it did scramble for a few ties. Better luck next time.

UEFA EURO 2020 HOST CITIES

For Euro 2020, it was decided that they would try something different. Instead of a solo host country, the idea of having multiple hosts was proposed, forming what has turned out to be a truly unified effort to host the illustrious tournament.

Here are the cities chosen to host UEFA Euro 2020:

Amsterdam, Netherlands
Baku, Azerbaijan
Bilbao, Spain
Bucharest, Romania
Budapest, Hungary
Copenhagen, Denmark
Dublin, Ireland
Glasgow, Scotland
London, England
Munich, Germany
Rome, Italy
Saint Petersburg, Russia

Mascot: Skillzy

What a great name for a mascot, Skillzy. He's got the skillz that thrillz.

The Stadiums

Amsterdam, Netherlands
Johan Cruyff Arena (which also goes by the spelling of Johan Cruijff ArenA)
Holds close to 55,000

Baku, Azerbaijan
Baku Olympic Stadium
Holds around 68,700

Bilbao, Spain
San Mamés
Holds a little over 53,000

Bucharest, Romania
Arena Naţională
Holds a little over 55,500

Budapest, Hungary
Puskás Aréna
Holds right around 67,889

Copenhagen, Denmark
Parken Stadium
Holds just a touch over 38,000

Dublin, Ireland
Aviva Stadium
Holds around 51,000

Glasgow, Scotland
Hampden Park
Holds around 51,800

London, England
Wembley Stadium
Holds a ball park range of 86,000-90,000 depending on the type of soccer match

Munich, Germany
Allianz Arena
Holds approximately 70,000-75,000 depending on the type of soccer match

Rome, Italy
Stadio Olimpico
Holds a little over 70,500

Saint Petersburg, Russia
Krestovsky Stadium
Holds somewhere around 56,000 with room for more depending on the type of event

UEFA EURO 2020 TEAMS

FRANCE

Euro Cup: 2
World Cup: 2
Overall Team Rating: 9.8

Known For
Strong attendance
Very passionate fans
Exciting games
Long history of high-quality football
Elite talent
Two UEFA Euro championships
Two World Cup championships
Michel Platini
Didier Deschamps
Zinedine Zidane
Henry
Antoine Griezmann
Mbappé

A BRIEF TEAM HISTORY

The defending World Cup champs enter the 2020 UEFA Euro with a plethora of past accomplishments. France's first World Cup championship arrived in 1998, when the team was led by Zinedine Zidane. The second title, of course, arrived in 2018.

France has done very well in recent UEFA Euro competitions. Let's take a step back for a moment and look at France's overall UEFA Euro record.

In 1960, France placed fourth. Not bad.

However, France didn't compete in 1964, 1968, 1972, 1976, and 1980.

Then, all of a sudden, out of nowhere, with the help of Platini, France won the 1984 Euro, a tournament that it happened to host that year. It was pretty impressive to jump straight from not competing to winning the whole thing. Platini, the team's star midfielder, had a phenomenal tournament, scoring 9 goals (which outdid all others that year). He later went on to become President of UEFA. As for his track record there, don't ask. A long time ago, he had a slight mix up with Sepp Blatter—the former longtime President of FIFA. It was a tiny little story that only happened to turn into one of the biggest corruption scandals in world sports history. (You remember that whole thing, it was buried on the back of page nine.) As it turns out, Platini is still being questioned about illicit international soccer affairs that happened some years ago, circa 2015, when he was in charge of UEFA. On June 18, 2019, *The Wall Street Journal* published, "Former French soccer star and high-ranking soccer administrator Michel Platini was detained in

Paris following a corruption investigation by French authorities into the awarding of the 2022 World Cup hosting rights to Qatar."[1] He continues to face the music as investigators have been trying to resolve the situation. Will Platini eventually wind up in a prison cell? Who knows? Let's face it, during his time at Juventus, his old team's uniform came across like an old-school prison outfit; perhaps his time there was a hint at things to come. Though, as a player, it should be pointed out, Platini was one of the best. His association with the aforementioned corruption scandal is partly why the story has been (and likely will continue to be) such big news. But, back in 1984, it was a different time altogether as Platini and France were champions of Europe.

In 1988, it was back to the drawing board because France didn't compete.

As for 1992, France qualified for the UEFA Euro but couldn't escape its group.

In 1996, France did well and made it to the semi-finals.

The UEFA Euro of 2000 was a big year for France. Zinedine Zidane and company lifted the championship trophy, making it France's second Euro title. This alone was a remarkable accomplishment, but France had also just won the 1998 FIFA World Cup, which made it all the more impressive.

The next few tournaments represented decent results for France.

In 2004, it reached the quarter-finals.

In 2008, France couldn't get out of its group.

As for 2012, it made the quarter-finals.

Most recently, in 2016, the French hosted the UEFA Euro and reached the final in which it lost to Portugal. In front of its home crowd, this wasn't the result that France had hoped for, but a second-place finish wasn't the worst thing in the world.

Can France keep the momentum going in 2020? It's a good question and one that will be answered in due time. France, the current World Cup champion, definitely will be a favorite. Whether or not it will win the UEFA Euro again is yet to be seen. If it does, it will be the first one since 2000. And, more importantly, it would make a grand total of three Euro titles.

FACTS ABOUT THEIR COUNTRY

Wine anyone? There are a few places on earth that are famous for the production of wine. You can't go wrong with the vineyards in Sonoma and Napa, California. Chile is well known for wine as well. Italy, top-notch. Spain as well. The list lingers on. However, arguably at the top of the wine list worldwide would be the aforementioned California locations along with France. While soccer is front and center as the pride of France, a few wineries that have distinguished French culture include Château Roubine, Château de Pitray, and Château Lafite-Rothschild.

The elegant French have won the UEFA Euro on two occasions, in 1984 (led by Michel Platini) and 2000 (led by Zinedine Zidane). In the FIFA World Cup department, France also has two titles from 1998 and 2018. The starting point really came in the late 1970s with the arrival of Michel Platini. Under his guidance from midfield, France nearly captured the 1982 and 1986 FIFA World Cups. Instead, he led France to a championship in the 1984 Euro, which France coincidently hosted. France also hosted the 1998 World Cup, which of course it won. There is something about France hosting where success just seems to follow. However, in the 2016 UEFA Euro, France hosted and came in second as it lost in the final to Portugal.

WHERE THE TEAM IS TODAY—TACTICS AND STRATEGIES

France is sitting on a grand opportunity to win yet another major tournament. It has the talent, experience, and the timing is just right. The 2018 FIFA World Cup champs are ready to go, with Mbappé leading the charge.

Tactics and strategies: Keep possession flowing, get the ball into center midfield often so it can be distributed throughout the field, which is something that France does very elegantly. This will enable the French to open up play downfield for optimal attacking results.

DIDIER DESCHAMPS—A BRIEF COACHING PORTRAIT

Didier Deschamps played midfield with a few different professional sides, including the likes of Nantes, Marseille, Bordeaux, Juventus, Chelsea, and Valencia. He was also a key member of the French championship team during the 1998 FIFA World Cup.

Can Deschamps guide France back to the UEFA Euro final? He has a talented team ready for the task, so it seems likely. France has been on a role. It won the 2018 FIFA World Cup and placed second in the 2016 UEFA Euro. Not bad. But that's not enough. France is aware of its talented team this year and definitely has its sights on a European championship. The pressure is on and if anything, Deschamps needs to keep his players focused. If the team can remain motivated to win, as opposed to falling prey to social distractions such as nightlife and drinking* (which is something any leading team has to contend with), then it should be on track to have a great tournament. If this is the case, the partying can wait until after the championship trophy has been lifted.

KEY PLAYERS AND THEIR CHARACTERISTICS

Mbappé, Antoine Griezmann, and Paul Pogba

Mbappé is hoping to live up to all the hype surrounding his astonishing run in the 2018 FIFA World Cup. The youngster, who plays for PSG, is ready to show the world that he is the best player in Europe. Whether or not this is true is another question. However, if France manages to win the 2020 UEFA Euro, and if Mbappé is instrumental, then he will definitely have an argument to make as the best player on the continent.

---

* When I owned a restaurant in California, my wine salesman, Francois, believed the 2002 French team lost the World Cup because they were drinking at night before games.

Antoine Griezmann will be leading France's cause with skill, timing, great passing, a will to score and the ability to be in the right place for scoring chances. He is a top-level talent with a lot of experience going into this tournament. France should be heavily leaning on him for production.

Paul Pogba is an interesting player. In some circles, he is a great talent, one you just can't do without. In other circles, he's highly overrated. Whichever opinion you share, he is one of France's leading players and will be guiding things from midfield in an all-out attempt to capture Europe's highest honor: the UEFA Euro.

Overall Player Rating:
Mbappé: 9.5
Antoine Griezmann: 9.5
Paul Pogba: 8.7

KEY PLAYER STATS

(Total career goals for their country)

	Games Played	Goals
Mbappé	34	13
Antoine Griezmann	78	30
Paul Pogba	69	10

WHAT TO WATCH FOR ON TV—HOW MBAPPÉ, RONALDO, AND OTHERS PLAY

Mbappé, Antoine Griezmann, and Paul Pogba will be leading the way for France.

Mbappé has the ability to jump all over opponents with bursts of speed that open up lanes downfield in attacking positions. His speed keeps opponents off-balance and allows France good scoring opportunities as a result. From the success of the 2018 FIFA World Cup, an article from *The Washington Post* commented on his young age: "It made sense that Mbappe would matter in the championship match of a World Cup in which he had introduced himself anew, even though soccer intellectuals have known of him since he made his professional debut for Monaco in 2015 at age 16 years, 347 days."[2] Now a few years on, France is eager to gain yet another major tournament title with its young star. The 2020 UEFA Euro is just within reach.

Luckily, for France's sake, there is yet another salient talent, Mr. Antoine. Antoine Griezmann adds a critical dimension to France's attack with skill, insight, and the ability to see the field with great vision. With him in the game, things just seem to happen in the best way.

Support players have the responsibility of working possession around the field with rhythm and accuracy; usually, in France's case, this is done at the highest level. The fluid, rhythmic passing was set into motion by Platini, years ago, and taken to a high art form under his guidance. (We can't forget Giresse and Tigana, among others, who made the game look so pleasant alongside Platini.) Zidane carried the torch during his playing days. Today, rest assured, each French player has been trained extensively with a certain French touch when it comes to the simple, yet complicated act of moving the ball around the field. The flow of France's passing can be a pleasure to watch for both aficionados and new viewers of the game. Keep an eye out for pure harmony in the passing game as France dances its way through the 2020 UEFA Euro.

WHAT ARE THEIR CHANCES OF WINNING THE EURO THIS YEAR?

Very good—top of the list.

Euro Cup: 0
World Cup: 1
Overall Team Rating: 9.5

Known For
Strong attendance
Very passionate fans
Exciting games
Long history of high-quality football
Elite talent
One World Cup championship
Bobby Charlton
Bryan Robson
Gary Lineker
David Beckham
Wayne Rooney
Harry Kane
Dele Alli
Jadon Sancho
Marcus Rashford
Raheem Sterling

A BRIEF TEAM HISTORY

Quite frankly, England, mighty England, hasn't had the best run in the UEFA Euro. "What? How's that?" you might ask. Now let's not forget that England's national team is a leader in world football, while at the same time the EPL has been sky-rocketing with success for as long as anyone can remember. What's more, the EPL is home to the majority of England's national team players. The Three Lions have even won the World Cup. However, for the UEFA Euro, don't ask. In fact, despite winning one World Cup title, when it comes to the World Cup and UEFA Euro, don't ask double-time. The topic conjures up too many emotional feelings that might cause a business man in good spirits to appropriate a bar stool for the next three hours, intermittently breaking out into a Morrissey vocal solo: "*So please, please, please, let me, let me, let me...let me get what I want this time.*" (Or something to that effect; courtesy of *The Smiths* but of course!) That has been the sentiment from the large contingent of English fans, generally speaking, for a long-long time. Speaking of intently following England in World Cup competition, Leo Robson wrote in *The New Yorker*, "But when England is, inevitably, knocked out—by the quarter-finals, in all likelihood—I will soon put it out of my mind and turn to the truly meaningful business of watching teams like Germany, Spain, and Brazil."[3] For England, pretty much across the historical spectrum from 1960 through 2016, the same scenario has always applied to UEFA Euros. (In terms of finding other teams to watch, Robson and others of his ilk might just replace Brazil with Italy or France.) The bottom line is pretty simple. In UEFA Euro competition, England—the inventors of the game and holders of one World Cup title from 1966—just can't catch a break. It has been a longstanding saga of defeat and disappointment. One can't deny, while England once dominated the world, it can't conquer Europe. Maybe someday.

This is part of the overall enigma of England's national team. True to form, as confusing as it may come across, aside from winning the 1966 World Cup, England hasn't had much luck in the UEFA Euro. In fact, saying that the previous statement is an "understatement" would be an insult to understatements everywhere.

For now, since we're on the topic, and what a mysterious one it is, let's take a quick glance at England's foray into Europe's highest tournament.

England didn't compete in the 1960 and 1964 Euros. Not a good start.

In 1968, the English placed third. A good result, but not the championship.

In 1972 and 1976, England didn't compete. Not exactly great.

In 1980, England didn't get out of the group stage. No good.

In 1984, England didn't compete. Oy vey.

In 1988 and 1992, again, it couldn't get out of its group. No good.

Then 1996 came around, and, lo and behold, watch out, England made the semi-finals and lost in a dramatic penalty shootout against Germany. Who was the player that missed the only penalty kick? England's current coach, Gareth Southgate. It just wasn't meant to be. A major disappointment for the English.

Southgate, who was a good player, now has a chance to make up for it as coach—an interesting turn of events. Will his team find itself in a penalty shootout? Maybe with Germany? Such a tale would be dramatic indeed. We'll just have to wait and see.

In 2000, England couldn't get past its group. Pretty disappointing.

In 2004, it got to the quarter-finals. A better result, but nowhere close to a championship.

England didn't compete in 2008, a big disappointment.

In 2012, it reached the quarter-finals.

Most recently in 2016, England made the Round of 16 where it lost to Iceland. No good.

Not much to write home about. No first place trophy. A lot of disappointment. Yet, when England has competed, it is always a contender which is partly why it's such an interesting side to watch.

Despite such a dismal record, England is one of the favorites in 2020 and this could be the year that history is made for the Three Lions.

FACTS ABOUT THEIR COUNTRY

England invented the game. The English national team dates back to 1872. It has one World Cup title from 1966. It also hosted that year, and the final game—which was against West Germany—was held in Wembley Stadium. However, England has zero Euro titles, which is surprising to many people considering the high level of soccer in England.

It's been a long time since England won the 1966 World Cup. As a result, England's fans are hungry for another title. Undoubtedly, during UEFA Euro 2020, win or lose, England's cities will be rocking with excitement. London is one of the world's elite major cities. Other cities of interest include Manchester, Liverpool, and Leeds.

England has long been a leader in world affairs. In all of world history, World War II stands out as one of the biggest events known to mankind. England (along with the United States, the Soviet Union, Germany, Italy, and Japan) was at center stage. Back in WWII days, Winston Churchill represented England in a famous meeting with President Roosevelt of the United States and Joseph Stalin of the Soviet Union. Prior to WWII, soccer was growing in popularity around the globe. In post WWII days, England has continued to lead in the world of soccer and hosts one of the world's best leagues, the English Premier League.

WHERE THE TEAM IS TODAY—TACTICS AND STRATEGIES

To say England has a good chance of winning this Euro 2020 would be a vast understatement. This isn't just a talented English team, it's a really talented one. This team is good. It's really good. I can't wait to see it in action. Fans around the world are eager to see how good England can be this time around. In fact, as most English fans are inclined to do, we should forget about past failures. This time around, it should be great. There is talent left and right. It's a team with experience and success from the 2018 FIFA World Cup. Liverpool, representing English soccer, just won the 2018-19 Champions League, and, as a result, English soccer is soaring again. It is flying high. How high? That is yet to be seen, but this 2020 Euro is just the right platform for England to prove its worth. Forget about the 2016 Euro and the embarrassing defeat to Iceland. Forget all about that. That was the past. This English squad has learned its lesson and sees big things for itself this UEFA Euro 2020 tournament. Though, as a side, England might just use the 2016 loss to Iceland—which was viewed with great intrigue by practically the whole planet—as motivation to prove itself on Europe's biggest stage.

Watch for frequent passing combinations with one and two touch soccer guiding the way.

Tactics and strategies: England will likely be using a 4-3-3, which allows any team to apply greater pressure defensively, as the players can cover more ground. It is a good lineup for the Three Lions as it also encourages possession play, for similar reasons. For starters, with a 4-4-2, it can be argued that the two forwards are too isolated and cannot cover enough ground as passes are being linked together. While, on the other hand, if you're operating out of a 4-3-3, the players have more ground covered, and, thus, can establish passes in a better manner. Should England stay with this formation, it will be a wise choice. England's players have phenomenal skill and technique. These virtues will be best displayed with a 4-3-3. Having said that, England needs to force the issue and put pressure on its opponents. While England is doing that, it needs to find a balance with long durations of possession, thus taking the game away from its opponents. Any time you have long durations of possession (or over-possession), it is a good thing. As a matter of fact, in a paradoxical way, it creates more scoring chances. Look for England to capitalize on such a thing. Doing so will be crucial for its success.

GARETH SOUTHGATE—A BRIEF COACHING PORTRAIT

Gareth Southgate was the player that missed the all-important penalty kick in the 1996 UEFA Euro shootout against Germany. This is something that he's probably thought about a million times. And, he's probably been reminded of it a million times too. He now has a unique opportunity to guide England to glory.

Back in 2016, Gareth Southgate signed a four-year agreement to coach England into the World Cup. In taking the job, he accepted all the pressure in the world, and he's more determined than ever to finally win the UEFA Euro, a tournament that has eluded England's grasp to this point. Southgate would be the very first, and such an accomplishment would make it into the history books of English soccer.

Born in 1970, Southgate's professional career (1988-2006) was spent playing with Crystal Palace, Aston Villa, and Middlesbrough. He also served as a longstanding member of the national team from 1995-2004, making 57 appearances.

His philosophy involves using strikers and outside midfielders down the line, crossing the ball—with proper service—from the wings with a firm backline that also has the aerial capability to stomp out opposing corner kicks, while serving as an asset on the offensive side of free kicks.

With Southgate at the helm, England's prospects are looking good. In fact, it did very well in World Cup 2018, placing fourth overall. Do not be surprised to see Southgate lead England to a 2020 Euro championship. He has a strong, talented team at his side, and there's no better time than the present.

KEY PLAYERS AND THEIR CHARACTERISTICS

Harry Kane, Dele Alli, Jadon Sancho, Marcus Rashford, and Raheem Sterling

Harry Kane, the Tottenham star, has stepped up as England's captain and a worthy one at that. He walked away from World Cup 2018 as the tournament's top scorer, and, most recently in Champions League competition, he helped Tottenham earn a second-place finish in the 2018-19 final (enduring a tough defeat to EPL rival Liverpool). In the Overall Player Rating, Kane received a relatively high score for what might otherwise be misconstrued as average play. Well, in fact, at first glance, Kane comes across as very average, though, over time, his overall gamesmanship is deserving of a 9.5. He is a scorer, he sets others up, and he has a great sense of where the ball should go. Kane, along with his crafty skill and keen awareness of positioning, will lead England toward the ultimate European quest for greatness: to hold the Euro trophy once and for all. It will be a challenging task, to say the least, but Kane certainly is optimistic about taking center stage and making a little English history along the way. His prospects are good. Along with his leadership ability and scoring prowess, England has its eye on the prize.

Kane's speed and quickness are below average, but he is deceptively effective at using both.

Dele Alli is a top-notch player to keep an eye on. He's a force in the midfield that gets things going and will be depended on for production up top, good transition play, distribution, and defensive responsibilities. Alli has good speed and quickness and endurance. These are assets that should help England late in games.

Jadon Sancho is, watch out, a super-skilled player making a name for himself with technique and dribbling prowess, along with a will to get around defenders. He will provide an attractive style of play while throwing around a few fancy moves here and there. With that said, if keeping a defense off-balance is a key to success, then England has a great opportunity to go far in this tournament with Sancho. He is very fast and quick, which are attributes that he uses well; as a result, defenders are often left wondering what just happened.

Marcus Rashford has good speed and represents a solid threat around goal. Without a doubt, Euro 2020 represents a great opportunity for him to stand out as one of Europe's best. Hopefully, for England's sake, he can place a few balls in the back of the net.

Raheem Sterling is quick, elusive and cunning. To say he's quick is an outrageous understatement. Perhaps lightning quick would be more appropriate. He provides an insane challenge for any defender unlucky enough to be guarding him. Can he be rattled? Yes. But, over the course of a game, should Sterling find a little space here and there, he can be counted on to create an optimistic scoring chance for himself or a waiting teammate. Sterling's strength resides in the ability to explore areas around the box. Though, in order to do this well, he relies on solid possession play from his teammates. There's a problem, however. If his teammates cannot get a good grasp on possession, it might indeed be difficult for Sterling to take matters into his own hands and carry the team with individual brilliance. In summary, good possession from England will induce advantageous situations for Sterling to show off his dangerous skills.

Overall Player Rating:
Harry Kane: 9.5
Dele Alli: 9.3
Jadon Sancho: 9.5
Marcus Rashford: 9.3
Raheem Sterling: 9.1

KEY PLAYER STATS

(Total career goals for their country)

	Games Played	Goals
Harry Kane	45	32
Dele Alli	37	3
Jadon Sancho	11	2
Marcus Rashford	38	10
Raheem Sterling	56	12

WHAT TO WATCH FOR ON TV—HOW MBAPPÉ, RONALDO, AND OTHERS PLAY

England, a national team that has been known for plenty of crosses in past years, is a group that combines crisp possession play with skillful insight in midfield and forward positions. While it always has a strong defense, one area of weakness would be its inability to provide offensive enlightenment from its defenders. Are England's defenders the worst options in the world? No, not at all, but they do lack a certain artistic ability on the offensive side of the ball that nations like Germany, Spain, and France have in abundance. For this tournament, this is no reason to put England in the doghouse. In fact, as always, England has a high chance of winning the whole tournament. It is really a matter of finding a good balance between strong defense and offensive ingenuity in all positions. If the chemistry in possession is good, then England should be on the right track. One area of concern will be if England has a hard time finding goals. If this is the case, England might resort to launching balls into the box with a hope and prayer (the old England). Though, if the players can remain calm and focus on strong possession buildup to create interesting chances around the box with improvisation, then England might just find itself in the winning seat.

Probably operating out of a 4-3-3, England is going to give it its best, and this might be the year it finally conquers Europe.

WHAT ARE THEIR CHANCES OF WINNING THE EURO THIS YEAR?

Very good—top of the list.

PORTUGAL

Euro Cup: 1
World Cup: 0
Overall Team Rating: 9.2

Known For
One UEFA Euro championship
Eusébio
Luís Figo
Nani
Cristiano Ronaldo

A BRIEF TEAM HISTORY

Let's take a quick glance at Portugal's journey in the UEFA Euro tournament.

Portugal didn't compete in the Euro tournament from 1960 through 1980. Yikes. Not a good start.

In 1984, Portugal made up for lost time, in a big way, by making the semi-finals in France. It was a decent result, but nowhere near a championship.

In 1988 and 1992, Portugal didn't compete. Not exactly great. In1996, things improved as Portugal made the quarter-finals. In 2000, things got even better for Portugal as it made the semi-finals. Not bad, but no championship yet.

The Euro of 2004 was a big year for Portugal as it earned second-place. As for 2008, Portugal made the quarter-finals. In 2012, it reached the semi-finals, a pretty good result.

Then came 2016. Who would've thought that Portugal would come out on top? Portugal had a good team but it's fair to say that outside of Portugal, not too many people predicted it would win the whole thing. Indeed, this was the year Cristiano Ronaldo and Nani would lead their country to the highest honor in Europe. Some people said, with much enthusiasm, that Portugal was not the best team in 2016. This would be true. However, to Portugal's credit, it fought hard and in the final game, which was against France, *in France*, it managed to pull out a win against a superior French side, even after its leader, Cristiano Ronaldo, left the game with an injury. This would be Portugal's biggest accomplishment to date. The team returns in 2020, looking to reassert its authority over the best in Europe.

FACTS ABOUT THEIR COUNTRY

Geographically speaking, Portugal is the epitome of Western Europe. It overlooks the Atlantic Ocean and has long been a seafaring country. Portugal is known for wine and is also a tourist destination. Without a doubt, soccer is the passion of the country's people. Portugal's national team dates back to 1921. After all this time, the 2016 UEFA Euro championship was the first of its kind for Portugal and represents the biggest athletic achievement the nation has earned so far.

WHERE THE TEAM IS TODAY—TACTICS AND STRATEGIES

Portugal has a lot to prove this tournament. It was not considered the best team in UEFA Euro 2016, even though it walked away with the trophy in hand.

Tactics and strategies: For all intents and purposes, Portugal will utilize Ronaldo's talents as much as possible. The team could use a little improvement in its defensive ball distribution. To be more specific, the defenders lack a little ingenuity in handling the ball during possession. Are they the worst in the world? No. But when it's all said and done, Portugal's possession game is not as precise as Germany's or France's. This has a lot to do with the defenders. Improvement in this category would be great for Portugal's chances to repeat as champions. When defenders are possessing the ball at the highest level, it allows the attacking players to be more productive.

Watch for Ronaldo to create danger in the attack with dribbling and surging runs around the box. He is getting a little older in soccer years but is still a major threat around goal. Portugal will look to get as much out of him as possible.

FERNANDO SANTOS—A BRIEF COACHING PORTRAIT

Fernando Santos was born in 1954 in Portugal. Since 2014, he has led Portugal and it has been a tremendous journey so far. To date, his biggest achievement with the team has been the 2016 UEFA Euro championship. It was an accomplishment of a lifetime. Now, he has the distinct honor of defending his country's title in 2020. All the pressure in the world is on him and his talented group of players. He and his team have to prove that they are worthy champions and a second consecutive title would be the best way to put critics to rest.

KEY PLAYERS AND THEIR CHARACTERISTICS

Cristiano Ronaldo, Bernardo Silva, Danilo Pereira, and João Félix

Cristiano Ronaldo is a multi-winning Ballon d'Or recipient with a coveted club career that has recently seen a big move from the renowned Real Madrid to Juventus. Along with winning multiple Champions League titles in the past, Ronaldo oversaw the 2016 UEFA Euro championship and is looking to bring home another. He's the biggest star Portugal has produced and one of the world's highest paid athletes. Where there's big money, there is usually skill, which Ronaldo definitely has plenty of. He's received plenty of criticism over the years, particularly for his whining after fouls. However, Ronaldo has reached a level of fame that few athletes in the history of sports have achieved and with that pressure one is certainly allowed to make a few blunders along the way.

He may be getting older in soccer years but he still has the ability to take over a game with dribbling and remarkable finishing around the box. Then, with direct kicks, he provides a dipping shot which has the ability to keep goalkeepers up at night. His speed, quickness, and strength are elite level.

Bernardo Silva brings midfield stability that has strengthened from his time with Manchester City. His distribution in midfield will be crucial for Portugal to find success and repeat as champions. Ronaldo and other attacking players will be depending on Silva for quality service throughout the field. His speed and quickness are good but not top of the list.

Danilo Pereira, who was born in 1991, is a midfielder that specializes in keeping things strong on defense. His contributions will be vital for Portugal to keep scores low. He currently plays domestically with Porto and has over 100 games to his credit. With Portugal, he has over 30 caps and this combined experience should be comforting for Portuguese fans as the team moves forward. He has good speed and quickness but nothing to write home about.

João Félix, born in 1999, is a young dynamic midfielder with a knack for getting around defenders which is setting him apart as a sought-after up-and-coming talent. He is a player to keep an eye on down the road. His presence as a rising star with Portugal could be the beginning of something great in Portuguese soccer. He is a little faster than you'd think, with good quickness as well.

Overall Player Rating:
Cristiano Ronaldo: 10
Bernardo Silva: 8.9
Danilo Pereira: 8.8
João Félix: 9

KEY PLAYER STATS

(Total career goals for their country)

	Games Played	Goals
Cristiano Ronaldo	164	99
Bernardo Silva	42	6
Danilo Pereira	37	2
João Félix	4	0

WHAT TO WATCH FOR ON TV—HOW MBAPPÉ, RONALDO, AND OTHERS PLAY

Probably operating out of a 4-4-2, Portugal has many weapons at its disposal, including Cristiano Ronaldo, Bernardo Silva, Danilo Pereira, and João Félix.

Portugal has interesting passing. It's constructive yet lacks the superiority of Spain, Germany, or France. While the defending

European champs are a good team, there is always a little something lacking from Portugal. It's a team that is typically always in contention yet just a step behind the previously mentioned Spain, Germany, and France in top-shelf quality across the board. Having said that, when we talk about Portugal, we're talking about the defending European champions. So go figure; it's an interesting juggling act Portugal presents.

Pepe, one the team's most well-known defenders, was born in 1983, so do the math: he's entering his late 30s. Maybe he won't be a huge factor this tournament. At the same time, his experience will be called upon as the team moves forward.

This is a team with talent, experience, skill, and an eye for greatness. It's a team looking to repeat as champions and it wouldn't be surprising to see such a thing occur. On this quest, Ronaldo is going to be front and center as the team's heart and soul of the offense. While this might be his last Euro, all eyes will be on his every move as he yields his tricky dribbling arsenal and aerial superiority on crosses. With a strong supporting cast, Ronaldo and coach Santos have a big opportunity to gather a second title.

WHAT ARE THEIR CHANCES OF WINNING THE EURO THIS YEAR?

Well, we'll see. However, at the end of the tournament, I don't expect to see a Portuguese celebration dance.

GERMANY

Euro Cup: 3
World Cup: 4
Overall Team Rating: 9.8

Known For
Strong attendance
Very passionate fans
Exciting games
Long history of high-quality football
Elite talent
Three UEFA Euro championships
Four World Cup championships
Franz Beckenbauer
Gerd Müller
Paul Breitner
Karl-Heinz Rummenigge
Pierre Littbarski
Rudi Völler
Lothar Matthäus
Jürgen Klinsmann
Miroslav Klose
Philipp Lahm
Bastian Schweinsteiger

Manuel Neuer
Mesut Özil
Thomas Müller
Toni Kroos
Marco Reus
Julian Draxler
Julian Brandt
Timo Werner

A BRIEF TEAM HISTORY

In 1960, 1964, and 1968 the West Germans didn't compete in the Euro.

In 1972, West Germany took home the title with a first place finish.

The following Euro in 1976 was a good result as well. Germany placed second. Not the championship, but most countries would be happy with that.

The Euro of 1980 was a great year for West Germany. It placed first. This was West Germany's second Euro title. Not bad. In three tournaments the Germans placed first, second, and first. Things slowed down a bit in 1984 as the West Germans couldn't escape the group stage.

In 1988, West Germany lost 2-1 in the semi-finals to the Dutch in a classic showdown. Euro 1992 was a better result for Germany as it placed second overall. Then 1996 came around and the Germans were back on top of Europe with its third Euro championship. In 2000 and 2004, Germany didn't do so well. In each tournament, it couldn't get past its group. Things got back on track in 2008 as Germany got second place that year. In 2012 and 2016, Germany reached the semi-finals and that was all she wrote to date.

Will UEFA Euro 2020 be another big year for Germany? The Germans certainly have a strong team—with Joachim Löw as coach—and the field of competition is wide open for a championship run.

FACTS ABOUT THEIR COUNTRY

Tourists tend to gravitate to Germany for food, beer, the Autobahn, and so much more. On behalf of *CNN,* Julyssa Lopez wrote, "Germany has been center stage through much of world history. Today, travelers head to the fascinating city of Berlin to get a firsthand look at remnants of 20th century events, such as World War II and the Cold War."[4] Germany has Berlin to offer along with many other interesting locations. Lopez added, "But even though the capital is the most popular tourist destination in the country, each of Germany's 16 states boast innumerable attractions: opulent palaces, rich forests, soaring mountains and picturesque villages."[5]

While tourists walk around enjoying a number of different things, there is no denying Germany's passion for soccer. Surely, any tourist would inevitably stumble across something soccer-related. Germany's national team dates back to 1908. Since then, it has been a long ride of success.

Germany has had the honor of having four World Cup championships and three UEFA Euro titles. Generation after generation, Germany has been a worldwide leader in soccer. It is the most popular sport and Germans appreciate a well-played game, that's for sure.

In terms of soccer gear, Germany also leads in worldwide production and distribution of two brands: Puma and Adidas. Puma still has a strong place in the soccer market, though, in previous years, it was much more of a mover and shaker. As a matter of fact, Puma was chosen by renowned stars like Pele and Maradona. Interestingly, in the early days of the USMNT, players such as John Harkes, Tab Ramos, Hugo Perez, and others, presumably had to wear Adidas, which sponsored the national team but instead chose to wear Puma on their own. The players even posed for a poster,* wearing Puma gear. However, throughout the generations, Puma has lost some of its allure. On the other hand, Adidas has remained on top alongside rival brand, Nike. A few leading players that have gone with Adidas include Messi and Mesut Özil. When big stars choose a particular brand, it reflects well upon that company. Certainly, Germany has been fortunate enough to be associated with Puma and Adidas all these years. Another plus for Adidas is that it has been recognized for its high-quality products; this opinion is shared pretty much across the board. Back in the early 1990s, the Copa Mundial soccer shoe was one of the most popular shoes around. Players knew that if the tag in the shoe said it was made

---

* As a kid I had that poster, which, along with a ton of other stuff normal people would throw away, I've kept all these years. Perhaps someday Mike and Frank from *American Pickers* will do a soccer-version of their show and drop by (wishful thinking, I'm afraid!).

in West Germany, then it was going to be even higher quality than a model made elsewhere. The leather was better, the feel of the shoe was better, and the touch on the ball was better; it was just better. An opinion, yes. But, generally speaking, when most people think Adidas, they think quality.

WHERE THE TEAM IS TODAY—TACTICS AND STRATEGIES

The Germans are expected to win. That's the bottom line. German fans have high expectations, and, quite frankly, everyone around the world expects big things from Germany.

Tactics and strategies: Keep possession going all game long. Should Germany relax and concentrate on possession, its natural overall soccer-playing dominance will create many scoring opportunities. Where there are scoring opportunities, there are goals and also saves by the keeper. That's how it goes. But more scoring opportunities is what Germany wants. And the best way to get there is to concentrate all efforts on sound possession soccer. Germany is at its best when it is completely dominating possession, which, by the way, it does very well. However, during the 2018 FIFA World Cup, which Germany would rather forget, there was a lack of fluidity in possession. Things seemed disjointed. The team appeared to be rushed. Things were just not flowing for the Germans, and the end result was atrocious. The great Germans did not even advance out of the group stage. Oy vey. This was especially not great for Germany, a leader in world soccer. The best way to get back on top, where Germany will certainly be again, is to readjust a few things here and there. One such thing is to re-concentrate all efforts on the approach to possession soccer and enjoying the ball again. It's a bit of a paradox, but true nonetheless: Once Germany forgets about scoring, more scoring opportunities will arise. Hence, a lot of possession will simply put Germany into good scoring positions.

Some people say, "Teams should go for it. Take chances. Go for goals. Trade punches. Get aggressive around the box. Speed up the flow of play." No. Stop it right now. While that is good, and should be the first instinct on a fast break, the teams should resort to possession when the fast break is not on. This is partly where Germany failed in the 2018 World Cup. Its possession game was rushed and things just got out of whack. Spain dominated Europe and the world from 2008-2012, winning the triple along the way. The Spanish did it with lots of possession. In fact, I don't think their opponents ever touched the ball. In its own way, Germany needs to dominate possession and good things will be around the corner.

JOACHIM LÖW—A BRIEF COACHING PORTRAIT

Joachim Löw, who led Germany to the 2014 FIFA World Cup title, has a great chance of capturing the 2020 UEFA Euro. With all his experience and expertise, which comes in the form of smart player positioning and an eye for good possession play, Löw has a phenomenal team ready to take the field. Under coach Löw, Germany will probably use a 4-3-3, although the team has also utilized a 3-4-2-1 and a 3-4-1-2 in the past. Rest assured, whatever the formation ends up being, Germany will be ready to play. Löw is very wise and German fans are counting on his soccer intellect to lead the team to the mountaintop.

KEY PLAYERS AND THEIR CHARACTERISTICS

Marco Reus, Julian Draxler, Julian Brandt, Timo Werner, and Toni Kroos

Marco Reus, a veteran attacking player from Borussia Dortmund, is ready for action. He has scored over 75 goals for his club and this is something Germany is counting on. With the national team, he has gathered over 40 caps and his experience should prove pivotal for Germany's success this tournament.

Julian Draxler, an attacking player with experience from Paris Saint-Germain, has over 50 games with Germany under his belt and will be called upon for solid contributions throughout the tournament.

Julian Brandt was born in 1996 and has been one of Germany's rising stars. He flourished at Bayer 04 Leverkusen for years and the star midfielder has skill, knowledge, good rhythm, and a will to win. He is one of Germany's best and should be a key player this tournament.

Timo Werner is a forward's forward. He has talent, speed, agility, and a strong ability to get the ball in the net. With RB Leipzig, the forward has been on a roll and goals just keep piling up. In the 2020 UEFA Euro, don't be surprised if Werner comes up big-time for Germany.

Toni Kroos is a veteran midfielder that Germany will depend on for significant leadership, accurate passing, field vision, and organization. His technical skill is top of the charts, and his soccer IQ follows suit.

Overall Player Rating:

Marco Reus: 9.3
Julian Draxler: 8.9
Julian Brandt: 9.4
Timo Werner: 9.4
Toni Kroos: 9.3

KEY PLAYER STATS

(Total career goals for their country)

	Games Played	Goals
Marco Reus	44	13
Julian Draxler	51	6
Julian Brandt	31	10
Timo Werner	29	11
Toni Kroos	96	17

WHAT TO WATCH FOR ON TV—HOW MBAPPÉ, RONALDO, AND OTHERS PLAY

Regardless of the formation, Germany will be highly structured in its positioning and spacing on the offensive and defensive sides of the ball (no surprise there). In terms of technique, the passing is of the highest order from practically every player; the passing combinations are top-shelf as well. Dribbling is subtly thrown in with great effect, however, Germany's passing will usually stand out the most. The Germans will riddle the field with passes, thus taking the game away from whoever is playing defense. More often than not, Germany outthinks, outperforms, and outworks its opponents. It is just the name of the game when Germany plays, and you can expect a victory each and every time. This is why the nation has acquired four World Cups and three UEFA Euros to date (which places Germany among the world's elite soccer programs). A few players to watch during the 2020 UEFA Euro include Leroy Sane, who plays with Manchester City, Serge Gnabry, Kai Havertz, Joshua Kimmich, Toni Kroos, and Leon Goretzka will be a handful for any other team.

The combination of Reus, Brandt, and Werner is tantalizing. If you are Germany and you have these three players alone, then things are looking good for you. Even if one of those players came off the bench, things are in good hands. A virtue of being the German national team is that there is plenty of depth in the lineup. Germany is one of those countries that could field a "B Team" that would have a good chance of winning a World Cup or UEFA Euro. Only a few countries in the world have this distinction. Brazil, Argentina, and Italy would be a few others. While it is true that the Germans had an atrocious 2018 FIFA World Cup, it really was about time. After all, along with Brazil, Germany leads the world with World Cup accomplishments. Sometimes a great soccer-playing nation needs a terrible tournament in order to press reset and put things into perspective. Germany has done that and is now ready to move forward. For all intents and purposes, Germany has regrouped from 2018 and is looking to seize every opportunity to make a statement in this 2020 Euro. The end result: Watch out Europe. You're probably looking at the 2020 Euro champions. Perhaps the only team stopping Germany would be itself. If there are no goals right away, the Germans shouldn't get frustrated. It would be in Germany's best interest to enjoy possession and reassert its creative pulse on the field. By enjoying possession, the Germans will eventually get more quality scoring chances. Psychologically, a top team like Germany is expected to score many goals, which is a burden for many top teams. With expectations like this, the players can get frustrated with low scoring games, which, in turn, influences the overall play on the field. Rather, if Germany falls in love with possession again, it will assert its natural ability to dominate opponents and create more scoring opportunities. Throughout the duration of a tournament, this is the best avenue for Germany.

WHAT ARE THEIR CHANCES OF WINNING THE EURO THIS YEAR?

Top of the list.

THE NETHERLANDS

Euro Cup: 1
World Cup: 0
Overall Team Rating: 9.3

Known For
One UEFA Euro championship
Being one of the best teams to never win a World Cup
Excellent passing
Long history of high-quality soccer
Johan Cruyff
Ruud Gullit
Frank Rijkaard
Ronald Koeman
Marco van Basten
Ronald de Boer
Frank de Boer
Ruud van Nistelrooy
Arjen Robben
Memphis Depay
Ryan Babel
Matthijs de Ligt
Georginio Wijnaldum
Virgil van Dijk

A BRIEF TEAM HISTORY

The Netherlands: a true soccer savant. However, its little escapade with the UEFA Euro has been somewhat less than spectacular. The one true exception would be 1988. Outside of that, things have been, let's just say, relatively good.

From 1960-1972, the Netherlands didn't compete in the UEFA Euro which wasn't a good start.

In 1976, the Netherlands jumped right in and got third place. Now we're talking.

In 1980 and 1984, the Netherlands didn't compete in the UEFA Euro. Well, back to, you know, not so good.

All right, here we go. In 1988, it was a different story. Led by Ruud Gullit, Marco van Basten, and Frank Rijkaard, the Netherlands took first place in the Euro. In the semi-finals, the Dutch had an epic showdown with West Germany on German soil. It was a much-anticipated match, one that saw two penalty kicks, making the score 1-1. Then, with time running out, Marco van Basten sent home the winning goal. In the final, the Soviet Union, a very good team that year, fell to the Dutch by a score of 2-0 with a goal from Gullit and a marvelous volley from, you guessed it, van Basten (it was a goal that appeared lucky and brilliant at the same time). The Dutch, led by coach Rinus Michels, a true master of the game, reigned supreme and celebrated its first major title.

In the next 20 years or so, the Netherlands did well but couldn't find the championship trophy. In 1992, the Netherlands made the semi-finals. Pretty good. In 1996, it made the quarter-finals. Not bad. In 2000 and 2004, it made the semi-finals.

In 2008, the Netherlands made the quarter-finals. In 2012, it didn't get out of the group stage. A tough result. In 2016, it didn't compete. No good. The Netherlands is back and ready for the 2020 UEFA Euro.

FACTS ABOUT THEIR COUNTRY

The Netherlands is a coastal nation in Western Europe known for waterways, boat-making, and a street party you may or may not have heard of. As Jeff Scott of *CNN* wrote, "Every April, the Dutch host the biggest street party in Europe. Previously Koninginnedag (Queen's Day), the festival is now Koningsdag (King's Day) in honor of King Willem-Alexander."[6] Should the Netherlands win UEFA Euro 2020, there will be celebrating in the streets like nobody's business. Oddly enough, as renowned as Dutch soccer is around the world, the Netherlands has only one major championship: the 1988 UEFA Euro. It hasn't won the World Cup but has placed second on three occasions: 1974, 1978, and 2012.

The Dutch national team soccer program dates back to 1905 and to this day exudes high quality passing.

WHERE THE TEAM IS TODAY— TACTICS AND STRATEGIES

Regardless of which year it is, just be sure to watch out for Dutch passing. The Netherlands is a nation known for producing players with elite technique and skill. On top of that, the players combine elite passing combinations. Coaches from around the world have learned such combinations from the Dutch. In effect, the Dutch have exported its training techniques around the world. One might think that by doing such a thing, the secrets are out and opposing teams can take advantage of the Dutch tactics. This might be true. However, if the team can concentrate its talents in the formula of passing, then good things should arrive for the Dutch.

Tactics and strategies: As usual, the Netherlands should concentrate on passing around its opponents and drive home wins from there. This is a team and program that exudes high-quality passing. The Netherlands will live and die by its passing ability.

RONALD KOEMAN—A BRIEF COACHING PORTRAIT

Ronald Koeman, a great central defender in his day, helped to lead the Netherlands to a 1988 UEFA Euro title. Some of his strengths as a player included technical ability, organization, along with a high soccer IQ. He also played club ball with Barcelona, along with a few others. His fingerprints are all over the current team; fans will see strong passing combinations and smart play at the highest level. As coach, it will be Koeman's greatest goal to achieve a UEFA Euro title to go along with his previous honor as a player.

KEY PLAYERS AND THEIR CHARACTERISTICS

Memphis Depay, Ryan Babel, Matthijs de Ligt, Georginio Wijnaldum, and Virgil van Dijk

Memphis Depay is an attacking player to be cautious of if you're the opposing team. He will combine skill, quickness, and speed to drive home goals. Keep an eye out for Depay this tournament as he could potentially have a great showing.

Ryan Babel has bounced around a little bit with club teams; he has spent time with Ajax and Liverpool, among others. He has also been around for a while with the national team of the Netherlands; he has gathered over 55 caps and the crafty winger will provide lots of skill and energetic runs with the ball to keep opponents off-balance.

Matthijs de Ligt—who was born in 1999—has stepped up as captain of Ajax, and now is the future of the Dutch national team. From defense, the confident youngster will be tasked with leading the team with smart passing, which will help the team establish itself in the long run. He was part of Ajax's great 2018-19 UEFA Champions League adventure and is looking to have a strong UEFA Euro 2020 tournament.

Georginio Wijnaldum is a midfielder with over 50 caps for his country and will be counted on for his experience and skill to push the Netherlands past opponents throughout the tournament.

Virgil van Dijk is just plain good. As a leading defender in the world, this Liverpool standout, who placed second in the 2019 Ballon d'Or voting behind Messi, is a stronghold for the Netherlands; much of the team's success will be pushed forward by the 6'4" van Dijk.

Overall Player Rating:
Memphis Depay: 9.3
Ryan Babel: 9
Matthijs de Ligt: 9.4
Georginio Wijnaldum: 9
Virgil van Dijk: 9.5

KEY PLAYER STATS

(Total career goals for their country)

	Games Played	Goals
Memphis Depay	52	19
Ryan Babel	63	10
Matthijs de Ligt	23	2
Georginio Wijnaldum	62	18
Virgil van Dijk	33	4

WHAT TO WATCH FOR ON TV—HOW MBAPPÉ, RONALDO, AND OTHERS PLAY

What a team coach Koeman has. Dutch soccer is definitely back on the scene. Some exciting players to watch out for include Ryan Babel, Memphis Depay, Matthijs de Ligt, Georginio Wijnaldum, and Frenkie de Jong. Let's not forget Donny van de Beek, a midfielder with experience from Ajax. Donny van de Beek was born in 1997 in the Netherlands. In the 2018-19 Champions League competition, he was one of the youngsters that led Ajax to a great tournament. Then, without a doubt, you have Virgil van Dijk, who finished as runners-up for the 2019 Ballon d'Or.

It's a very strong group that could make huge waves this tournament. Watch for crisp passing. All passes are a joy to watch because the players have exquisite technique. If you combine this with a high soccer IQ, you have a formidable group that is very excited about the prospects of adding a second UEFA Euro title to its trophy case back in the KNVB headquarters.

The Netherlands will most likely operate out of a 4-2-3-1 and are a team to watch for sure. In fact, a team to watch is a vast understatement. They are a must-see. The Netherlands is back.

WHAT ARE THEIR CHANCES OF WINNING THE EURO THIS YEAR?

Very good. Don't be surprised to see the Netherlands standing with the first place trophy.

BELGIUM

Euro Cup: 0
World Cup: 0
Overall Team Rating: 9.4

Known For
Jan Vertonghen
Eden Hazard
Kevin De Bruyne

A BRIEF TEAM HISTORY

Belgium has had an interesting relationship with the UEFA Euro tournament.

In 1960, 1964, and 1968, Belgium didn't compete in the UEFA Euro. Not a great start.

Then, in 1972, lo and behold, the Belgians showed up out of nowhere and placed third overall. A great result for a team that arrived for the first time.

Then in 1976, it was back to the drawing board as Belgium didn't compete.

Well, in true Belgian form, the 1980 UEFA Euro saw Belgium place second overall. Just like that. There was a subtle trend developing. For the first three tournaments, Belgium didn't compete. Then, all of a sudden, it placed third. Then Belgium didn't compete again, followed by a second place finish. Huh?

However, things went downhill from there. In 1984, Belgium qualified but couldn't get past the group stage.

In 1988, 1992, and 1996, Belgium didn't compete.

In the 2000 UEFA Euro, Belgium was back and couldn't get out of its group.

And then, yet again, in 2004, 2008, and 2012, Belgium didn't compete. Wow.

The 2016 UEFA Euro was a different story as Belgium fielded a good team and made it to the quarter-finals.

Despite all its efforts, a first-place finish in the UEFA Euro has eluded Belgium. With a strong team in place, albeit a team with potential to be extraordinary, Belgian fans are hoping that 2020 will be a legendary year. These fans—Belgians from across the small geographical boundary that is Belgium, along with fans scattered around the world—are united and in good spirits and feel that if there is ever a time to make a run at a championship, it is 2020.

FACTS ABOUT THEIR COUNTRY

To date, Belgium has not won the UEFA Euro or World Cup. For a national team that dates back to 1904, there have been some good showings but no major titles just yet.

The best-known Belgian city would arguably be Brussels. However, wherever you might go, you are most likely to encounter some well-known Belgian beer because Belgium is all about good brew. Meredith Bethune of *CNN* wrote, "Beer aficionados around the world flock to Belgium for its internationally renowned brews."[7] Belgium's rather small geography allows visitors easy access to experience a long history of beer production. According to Meredith Bethune, "The tiny country of less than 12,000 square miles has more than 800 years of experience—monks first began brewing behind abbey walls back in the 12th century."[8]

A few recognizable beers include Stella Artois, Duchesse De Bourgogne, Duvel Tripel Hop, and Chimay Triple.

WHERE THE TEAM IS TODAY— TACTICS AND STRATEGIES

Belgium—sporting red, white, black, and yellow—has so many weapons on the field that it's hard to imagine it not getting to the semi-finals. However, over the years, a UEFA Euro title (and the World Cup while we're at it) has always seemed to elude Belgium.

Tactics and strategies: Get outside defenders involved in the attack more often. Belgium got a 9.4 Overall Rating because, in part, its defenders don't contribute to the offensive end of things as much as they could. Top class, yes, but, some improvements on the offensive side of the ball would push Belgium's quality up a couple notches.

Generally speaking, if Belgium uses a 3-4-2-1, which it has used in the past, then it's asking for trouble. Using three defenders is never a good move, no matter how you balance it out with midfield help. I would suggest tossing this lineup out and starting fresh with four defenders, maybe five.

ROBERTO MARTINEZ—A BRIEF COACHING PORTRAIT

Roberto Martinez, who is originally from Spain, coached Everton from 2013-2016. He took over Belgium in 2016.

As a player, Martinez was a defensive midfielder that played with a spell of teams, including Wigan Athletic and Swansea City.

His Spanish background is serving the Belgians well; he's implemented a passing structure that allows the stars a lot of room to go at defenders. Under his guidance, Belgium finally has a chance to win a major tournament.

KEY PLAYERS AND THEIR CHARACTERISTICS

Jan Vertonghen, Eden Hazard, and Kevin De Bruyne

Jan Vertonghen is a veteran defender that is a good tackler with plenty of skill on the ball to boot. Can he dribble away from annoying forwards? Yes. Does he have excellent passing ability? Yes. He's a great piece on the board if you're Belgium.

Eden Hazard, a renowned attacking player who gained experience with Lille, Chelsea, and Real Madrid, dribbles like nobody's business. He's quick and darts around like an elite dribbler should. An article from *USA TODAY* pointed out, "As Eden Hazard blossomed into one of the most dominant soccer players in the world, he admits he still occasionally found time to play FIFA, the popular video game, with friends and teammates."[9] At times, his dribbling—the maneuvering and quickness—comes across like a video game. Defenders have a mess of a time keeping up with him. Anytime he's on the ball, it is high-octane excitement and must-see football theater. Does he keep defenders off balance? That's an understatement. Does he create brilliant passes to teammates? Yes and very well. He's also a scorer and one of Europe's top players for good reason.

Kevin De Bruyne signed with Manchester City in 2015. He has done well in England and the attacking midfielder has also represented Belgian football extremely well. He provides excellent skill and technique with a good eye for goal. Considering all of his experience, skill, and willingness to win, he's a great asset for Belgium this tournament.

Overall Player Rating:
Jan Vertonghen: 9.4
Eden Hazard: 9.8
Kevin De Bruyne: 9.5

KEY PLAYER STATS

(Total career goals for their country)

	Games Played	Goals
Jan Vertonghen	118	9
Eden Hazard	106	32
Kevin De Bruyne	74	19

WHAT TO WATCH FOR ON TV—HOW MBAPPÉ, RONALDO, AND OTHERS PLAY

Probably operating out of a 3-4-2-1, Belgium will excel at passing from side to side, fluid passing connections, along with brisk counterattacks. Meanwhile, there will be energetic dribbling runs from attacking players such as Eden Hazard and Kevin De Bruyne, with Jan Vertonghen holding down the defense. It should all come together from the vision of coach Martinez by way of wearing down opponents with high quality soccer from end to end. Of course, if you have Thibaut Courtois in goal, then you're in good hands. Expect to see Belgium keep scores low thanks to its good defense and goalkeeping, whereas it should likely tally up a number of goals on its quest for the cup.

WHAT ARE THEIR CHANCES OF WINNING THE EURO THIS YEAR?

Quite good. Belgium has an extremely talented group of players and is looking to take advantage of this. However, the one thing holding Belgium back is the fact that it still has never won a major title, which could have a psychological impact and therefore hinder the team. On top of this, Belgium has a great squad, but thanks to injuries and Father Time, it's one that will eventually run out of steam and lose its top players (including but not limited to Eden Hazard and Kevin De Bruyne). This adds extra pressure for Belgium because the players feel like they have to "win now or never," which creates a considerable amount of stress. And stress tends to result in constrained performances. For this reason, unfortunately for Belgian fans, Belgium will probably not win the 2020 UEFA Euro.

ITALY

Euro Cup: 1
World Cup: 4
Overall Team Rating: 9.3

Known For
Strong attendance
Very passionate fans
Exciting games
Long history of high-quality football
Elite talent
Good defense
One UEFA Euro championship
Four World Cup championships
Bruno Conti
Paolo Rossi
Franco Baresi
Paolo Maldini
Roberto Donadoni
Roberto Baggio
Demetrio Albertini
Andrea Pirlo
Fabio Cannavaro
Francesco Totti

Gennaro Gattuso
Daniele De Rossi
Giorgio Chiellini
Lorenzo Insigne

A BRIEF TEAM HISTORY

Italy's success dates back to the golden era of early soccer. True to form, the Italians dominated world soccer in the 1930s by winning two World Cup championships. Since then, Italy has tallied up two more World Cups, from 1982 and 2006 respectively.

Italy also won the 1968 Euro title. Quite a trophy case. As for the UEFA Euro, let's take a look at Italy's overall record.

In 1960, during the opening Euro tournament, it may come as a surprise, Italy didn't compete.

As for 1964, ditto.

Then, as confident as ever, the Italians marched to a championship at the 1968 Euro, as if to say, "Who needs the first two tournaments? We're here now; the trophy's ours; you're welcome."

Then, oddly enough, for 1972 and 1976 Italy didn't compete.

In 1980, Italy was back and placed fourth overall.

Then, in 1984, you may have guessed by now, Italy didn't compete. (As good as Italy is, Europe's a tough backyard to have success in.)

The Italians were back in 1988 but it wasn't meant to be. However, Italy did make it to the semi-finals where it lost to the Soviet Union.

In 1992, Italy didn't compete.

In 1996, Italy showed up but couldn't escape its group.

The Euro of 2000 was a good result. Italy placed second as it lost to France in the final. It wasn't the first-place finish Italy had hoped for, however, it was better than every other tournament since 1968.

The Euro of 2004 wasn't particularly memorable for Italy. A great year would have seen Italy lift the championship trophy. A decent year would have seen Italy reach the quarter-finals. In this particular year, the final outcome was that Italy couldn't get out of its group. Back to the drawing board.

In 2008, Italy did better and reached the quarter-finals.

In 2012, Italy made the final match, yet again, but failed to lift the coveted Euro trophy as it lost to Spain.

Most recently, in 2016, Italy made the quarter-finals and that was it. Given its track record, don't be surprised in the least to see Italy win the 2020 UEFA Euro. It had a strong qualification run to arrive in the tournament and things are only looking good for the Italians at this point.

FACTS ABOUT THEIR COUNTRY

Italy boosts four World Cup titles and one Euro. Not bad. Rome is the capital and is known for many historical things. However, there is one place that particularly stands out. Writing for *CNN*, Bija Knowles captured one of the world's most popular places: "Rome's most photogenic landmark, the Colosseum looks good from just about all angles, even from below ground. You can see for yourself if you visit one of the tunnels (where gladiators waited before a fight), which have been opened to the public in recent years."[10] Whereas gladiator "activities" might have consumed the attention of passionate Roman fans over a thousand years ago, in today's Italy, soccer, without a doubt, is the passion of the land. Though, A.S. Roma does not have the best team in the land, neither does A.C. Milan in the north or Napoli in the south. Juventus is currently Italy's leading club team; it has been racking up Serie A titles in record fashion and doesn't seem to be stopping anytime soon.

Who are a couple legendary Italian national team players? Oy vey, there are too many. Dino Zoff, Bruno Conti, Paolo Rossi, Franco Baresi, Paolo Maldini, Roberto Donadoni, Roberto Baggio, Andrea Pirlo, and Fabio Cannavaro immediately come to mind, but the list goes on and on.

WHERE THE TEAM IS TODAY—
TACTICS AND STRATEGIES

Italy is ready for a strong showing in the 2020 UEFA Euro. In fact, it's a nation looking to recharge its reputation after recent international failures.

Tactics and strategies: Strong defense, as usual. Italy has been in a lull of late. It hasn't lived up to the well-known Italian standard that has been established over past years. Somehow, someway, Italy needs to regroup and find its winning ways again. On route to this goal, you can rest assured that Italy will have a strong defense. This is true and should remain Italy's top priority. However, where Italy has lacked progress in recent times has been on the offensive side of the ball. To be more specific, Italy's creativity has virtually been thrown out the window. While Italy maintains a strong defense, it should definitely look to improve on the creative side of things, although this is easier said than done. Though, despite being known for defense, one of the paradox's regarding Italy's game is that it has always been a very creative side. Indeed, when the Italians have the right pieces on the board, with the offense flowing in harmony, there is practically no stopping the Azzurri. And, when Italy has a unified offensive team, it's a thing of beauty. While Italy gets back on track, concentrating on strong defense will be and should be its focus. This will give the Italians some wiggle room as the offensive issues get sorted out.

ROBERTO MANCINI—A BRIEF COACHING PORTRAIT

Roberto Mancini, a former forward with experience on Italy's national team, has a strong task ahead to keep Italy afloat in this competitive 2020 UEFA Euro. As a coach, he has guided Inter Milan and Manchester City, among others. Italy did very well in qualifying for UEFA Euro. In October of 2019 *The Washington Post* reported, "Mancini has got Italy back on track, nearly two years after the Azzurri's embarrassing failure to qualify for the World Cup."[11] He currently is the man for the job to guide Italy to greatness. It is a responsibility that comes with a lot of pressure, the likes of which are unique to Italy, England, Brazil, Argentina, and a few other nations, to say the least. Italians love their soccer and the coach feels the force of each loss. Hopefully, for Mancini's case, there will be less losses and more wins as he pushes his team forward in a 4-3-3. While the formation might change from time to time, Italy's passion for greatness will not, and Mancini will be front and center for an important Italian adventure in the 2020 UEFA Euro.

KEY PLAYERS AND THEIR CHARACTERISTICS

Lorenzo Insigne, Giorgio Chiellini, Leonardo Bonucci, Marco Verratti, and Jorginho

Lorenzo Insigne is a skillful threat up top that Italy is counting on for plenty of goals. Is he Paolo Rossi? Or Gerd Müller? Well, that remains to be seen. The UEFA Euro is one of the best stages to lift your reputation to the level of such great scorers from the past.

Giorgio Chiellini is a highly experienced defender with over 100 caps for Italy. He should actually receive a lower score for his Overall Player Rating if not for his experience and leadership ability. The problem with good old Chiellini is that he doesn't offer much panache on the offensive side of the ball. Good defender? Yes. But he lacks technical ability with the ball and the ability to lead the attack with instrumental passes. He is no Franco Baresi, that's for sure. But he is a good defender that brings a solid presence with a ton of experience to the table. For the sake of Italian soccer, he is an example of how Italy holds on to beloved players for too long. Another one that comes to mind would be Pirlo, not to mention Buffon. It once seemed that Pirlo was never leaving the team. All three players deserve to be Italian legends, but when you hold on to them for too long, it doesn't allow room for up-and-coming talent to gain valuable experience with the team. However, there's value in having experienced players like Chiellini and Pirlo on the field. It is a delicate balance that Italy needs to figure out sometime in the near future. For now, Chiellini (assuming the coach keeps him on the roster) is looking to guide his team into the championship game during this 2020 UEFA Euro, which will likely be his last.

Leonardo Bonucci has turned into one of Italy's best defenders in recent years. As a leader with Juventus and the Italian national team, Bonucci is an essential component for Italy's success in UEFA Euro 2020. Without him, Italy might have a hard time finding its way.

Marco Verratti, who has over 180 games under his belt with Paris Saint-Germain, will add value to the midfield as he surges forward in hopes to bring Italy goals and assists. This will be highly treasured work as Italy looks to bring home the first place trophy.

Jorginho, who was originally born in Brazil, is a midfielder with experience from Chelsea in the EPL that Italy is counting on for ball distribution from the center of the field. His role will be to gather the ball and move his side along with instrumental passes that bring together a harmony in possession. Italy, when playing at its best, excels in this regard. Hopefully, for Italy's sake, Jorginho can bring it all together for a finished product that is nothing less than spectacular.

Overall Player Rating:
Lorenzo Insigne: 9
Giorgio Chiellini: 8.6
Leonardo Bonucci: 9
Marco Verratti: 9
Jorginho: 9.2

KEY PLAYER STATS

(Total career goals for their country)

	Games Played	Goals
Lorenzo Insigne	34	7
Giorgio Chiellini	103	8
Leonardo Bonucci	95	7
Marco Verratti	36	3
Jorginho	22	4

WHAT TO WATCH FOR ON TV—HOW MBAPPÉ, RONALDO, AND OTHERS PLAY

Going up against Italy is always tough.

Probably operating out of a 4-3-3, Italy will go full-throttle at opponents with technique, team organization, some flair, and, without a doubt, strong defense. Italy has a way of pressuring opponents with zones and great one-on-one defending. Call it a knack. Most opposing attacks fade away like a forgotten dream.

In general, when playing at its best, Italy can blend offense and defense like few others. With a strong counterattack, the Italians pressure opponents from all angles. Leading the cause should be Lorenzo Insigne, Giorgio Chiellini, Marco Verratti, Jorginho, and Federico Bernardeschi, to name a few.

WHAT ARE THEIR CHANCES OF WINNING THE EURO THIS YEAR?

Very good. Italy is, after all, Italy. Never count Italy out. It is a nation that ranks at the top of the list for World Cup titles, with one Euro to its credit. Despite not doing very well in international tournaments recently, Italy is too good to ignore.

Euro Cup: 3
World Cup: 1
Overall Team Rating: 9.8

Known For
A long tradition of quality soccer
Very passionate fans
Amazing passing
Elite talent
Three UEFA Euro championships
One World Cup championship
Raúl
Xavi
Iniesta
David Villa
Puyol
Sergio Ramos
Sergio Busquets

A BRIEF TEAM HISTORY

Spain is one of the top-quality teams that has been very good for a long time. Despite not winning a World Cup for many years, Spain was a quality side. In actuality, it had a brief stint with success in one of the early Euro Cups in 1964, followed by a long string of zero major titles until 2008, when Spain earned its second Euro Cup. This was followed by its first World Cup title in 2010, and then a third Euro Cup in 2012. This feat, winning a Euro Cup, World Cup, and Euro Cup in a row (known as the Triple), has never been accomplished by any other European team. And, because it is such an amazing claim, it is hard to imagine that any team will repeat such a thing.

In regard to the UEFA Euro, Spain, whose soccer program dates back to 1920, has an interesting history.

For starters, Spain didn't compete in the 1960 Euro.

As for 1964, Spain won the whole thing thus earning its first major football title.

Then things went downhill a bit. From 1968 to 1976, Spain didn't compete in the Euro.

In 1980, Spain qualified but couldn't get past its group.

In 1984, Spain did much better and got second place overall.

In 1988, Spain couldn't get out of its group.

In 1992, Spain didn't compete.

Then in 1996 and 2000, Spain reached the quarter-finals.

As for 2004, Spain couldn't get out of its group.

Then magic started to happen. In 2008, Spain won the whole thing. This was followed by another magical run in 2012 in which Spain repeated as champion.

Most recently, in 2016, Spain got to the Round of 16 and that was it.

Spain's national team dates back to 1920, and here we are 100 years later. The UEFA Euro of 2020 is a great opportunity for Spain to embark upon another championship run. If it does, it will be the fourth Euro title for the Spaniards.

FACTS ABOUT THEIR COUNTRY

Spain loves its soccer. This is an understatement. As a country, Spain has had a lot to celebrate. It's a country that can flaunt one FIFA World Cup title from 2010 and three UEFA Euro titles from 1964, 2008, and 2012. Winning the 2008 Euro, 2010 World Cup, and 2012 Euro in a row set Spain apart from all European neighbors as the only nation to accomplish such a thing. In short, it was amazing and there is a strong chance that it will never happen again. During this time, when Spain achieved the Triple, its team was referred to as the Golden Generation.

During the Triple, who did Spain defeat in each championship? In the 2008 Euro, it was Germany. In the 2010 World Cup, it was Netherlands. In the 2012 Euro, it was Italy.

Madrid, beautiful and cosmopolitan, centrally located, represents Spain as the country's capital. It also hosts one of the best teams in the history of world club football, Real Madrid, which is currently coached by Zinedine Zidane. Spain's other most famous city, Barcelona, whose club team isn't too shabby either, is explained in brief by Ian Hawkey, writing for *CNN*, "It wants to be acknowledged in the travel world as more sophisticated than Madrid, more progressive than Paris and a great deal more efficient than Rome."[12] While Real Madrid and Barcelona battle it out for soccer supremacy, each club heavily contributes to the Spanish team whereby everyone in Spain unites for the sake of national pride and hopefully another trophy.

Spain is a producer of fine wine, and plenty of it. As for beer, Spanish fans have many options, including Estrella Galicia. During UEFA Euro 2020, Spanish fans watching the games from home will likely be partying through the night as their team looks to make history again. Seeing as Spain didn't do very well in the 2014 FIFA World Cup, Spanish fans are leaning on the 2018 World Cup, which was a vast improvement, as Spain navigates through Europe's best in UEFA Euro 2020.

WHERE THE TEAM IS TODAY— TACTICS AND STRATEGIES

Spain is in a position of trying to keep the old guard alive and well while implementing new players into the scheme. The old guard has essentially dwindled away. What's left consists of a few players from the famous bunch that took part in the Golden Generation years.

Tactics and strategies: Keep things moving in the same direction and hope to find goals.

Sergio Busquets and Sergio Ramos are carryovers from the Golden Generation. Alba is lingering with that crowd as well. Spain is essentially keeping the train going forward, trying its best to reduplicate all the success it had circa 2008-2012. Though without Xavi, Iniesta, and a few others, it will be difficult to actually win big tournaments. That is, Spain will be one of the favorites but it will have a hard time getting enough goals to bring home another major trophy. The previously mentioned leaders from the Golden Generation had a certain knack about dominating possession *and* getting goals. Also, the Golden Generation had a will to win, which is hard to teach anyone at any level. You either have it or you don't. This current Spanish team has the possession part of the game down, not to mention elite technical ability, but getting goals combined with a will to win might be a challenge that holds Spain back a little bit. Again, Spain will likely be a contender for the final match, or, say, the semi-finals, but winning the whole thing will probably not occur. However, with its sights on the trophy, Spain has an assortment of high-end talent that includes Isco, Rodrigo, and Álvaro Morata.

LUIS ENRIQUE—A BRIEF COACHING PORTRAIT

For a moment or two, Robert Moreno was big news. He is a former assistant coach with Barcelona and Spain. As of 2019, he took the job of head coach for one of the best teams in the world. It is no surprise that Spain is one of the world's elite, but to take the position of head coach for such a team is an honor and a challenge. He replaced Luis Enrique, who stepped down as Spain's coach. It turns out it was only temporary. Lo and behold, Enrique—a former standout for Real Madrid and Barcelona—resumed his role as coach for Spain (while Moreno ended up landing with Monaco in France). With Enrique back at the helm, the honor is obvious, and the challenge will be to meet the expectations set by Spain's Golden Generation. What kind of party will it be if he manages to get Spain a fourth UEFA Euro title? A big one to say the least. If Enrique can pull it off, he will be regarded as one of Spain's best coaches of all time. The 4-3-3 should serve him well on this journey for greatness. It's a formation that his team is comfortable with as it affords a possession-oriented side like Spain easy access to passing channels throughout the field. Should Enrique and Spain march to the final, the 4-3-3 and possession soccer will be leading the way—this is where Spain has found success in the past. Spain's ability to possess the ball at the highest level completely stifles opponents into submission. For the most part, this was the case during Spain's UEFA Euro 2020 qualifying run in Group F whereby Spain comfortably led the way. For this reason, any team in the way should watch out.

KEY PLAYERS AND THEIR CHARACTERISTICS

Isco, Sergio Busquets, Sergio Ramos, Álvaro Morata, and Rodrigo

Isco is an amazing technician of the ball. Each pass is perfectly placed, with touch and thought behind it. Watch as Isco lights up the tournament with brilliant play.

Sergio Busquets should be keeping everything organized in the center of the field. The midfielder used to be behind Xavi and Iniesta, providing them support with dependable passes to keep the play going. Now he is the guy in the middle with the responsibility of keeping Spain's juggling act of possession and success going in the right direction.

Sergio Ramos, captain of the team, leads defense with insight, experience, technical ability, leadership, and timely tackles. As the heart and soul of this lineup, he has been through the good years while also enduring the embarrassment of the 2014 World Cup, along with unfortunate departures in UEFA Euro 2016 and World Cup 2018. UEFA Euro 2020 is an opportunity for Ramos and company to regain first place as Europe's finest team. Not to mention, considering Ramos' age, this might be his last UEFA Euro tournament as a starter; the same goes for Busquets. This may motivate both players to elevate their games and in the process deliver Spain yet another trophy.

Álvaro Morata has a lot of quality club experience with Real Madrid, Juventus, Chelsea, and Atletico Madrid. He plans on bringing all this together on route to outright brilliance in the 2020 UEFA Euro. Is he up to the task? Can he help lead Spain to the championship podium? He is an important piece in the Spanish puzzle and will need to be at the top of his game if Spain is to have a chance.

Rodrigo was born in 1991 in the flamboyant Rio de Janeiro, Brazil. Usually found on the outside, he is an attacking player that Valencia depends on for goals; so far he's done pretty well with his club side, knocking in over 30 goals with his eyes on more. The pressure is on to transform his La Liga success over to the Spanish national team during UEFA Euro 2020. If he can lead Spain to a championship, he will likely be regarded as a true Spanish hero. If he fails, then he might just be viewed as some Brazilian guy.

Overall Player Rating:
Isco: 9.3
Sergio Busquets: 9.1
Sergio Ramos: 9.5
Álvaro Morata: 9
Rodrigo: 9

KEY PLAYER STATS

(Total career goals for their country)

	Games Played	Goals
Isco	38	12
Sergio Busquets	116	2
Sergio Ramos	170	21
Álvaro Morata	33	17
Rodrigo	22	8

WHAT TO WATCH FOR ON TV—HOW MBAPPÉ, RONALDO, AND OTHERS PLAY

Probably operating out of a 4-3-3, Spain will be taking possession soccer to new heights, yet again. Known throughout Europe and the rest of the world, Spain will take the game away from its opponents with possession on top of possession, which is a series of short passes commonly known as tiki-taka. For some, it's a pleasure to watch, for others it's boring. Wherever you fall, without a doubt, Spain will outplay most opponents with this tactic and keep the ball for a majority of the game. From my perspective, it's a thing of beauty. Scoring a goal is hard and mastering possession is even harder. All players need to be on the same page and flow together like a grand symphony, all while defenders are storming the stage trying to steal the instruments. Therefore, the amount of skill it takes for players to outmatch an opponent, not to mention the coaching that goes into it, is outstanding. It takes technical ability along with a high soccer IQ. My take is: Sit back, watch, and enjoy. It is brilliant.

While Spain has mastered possession, some of its key players that bring it about (players who are renowned throughout Spain as folk-legend-like heroes) would be Sergio Busquets, Isco, Sergio Ramos, and Jordi Alba, to name a few. Meanwhile, Jesús Navas, now on the outside helping with defense, has the wheels to run down just about anyone and if you have to chase him down, then you're just going to work for it.

The aforementioned Jordi Alba provides stability that is so crucial for Spain's success. As an outside player, he is vital in the overall progression of possession for Spain, which, as a team, works the ball from side to side frequently. When the ball reaches the outside positions, it's extremely important to have a smart player like Alba that can keep the flow going in the best way possible.

Francisco Alcácer García, also known as Paco, will be a forward to watch. He has a remarkable amount of goals with time on the national team already (17 in 12 games as of October 2019 leading into UEFA Euro 2020). Add to this, his experience with Borussia Dortmund and Barcelona and you have a winning combination on your hands.

Will Álvaro Morata and Rodrigo be enough up top to put in the valuable goals needed for Spain's fourth Euro title? Will Isco be creative enough in midfield to help in this endeavor? With the help of Ramos on the backline, and Busquets in midfield, it will be very interesting to see just how well the Spanish can do.

Busquets, Isco, Thiago, Saul, Ruiz, and Santi Cazorla provide formidable threats in midfield for any team. Spain is all about midfield play; there are so many mids to choose from which makes it hard for the coach to decide who to play during any given game. Sure, you have Busquets, Isco, and Thiago but there are any number of players that can get the job done. You could also throw a lesser known player like Daniel Parejo into the mix. Parejo was born in 1989 in Spain and has a little experience with the Spanish national team. Although with Valencia, he has gone over 260 games played, and counting. Outside of Valencia, Parejo, who it turns out is an experienced midfielder, has also spent time with Real Madrid, Queens Park Rangers, and Getafe. It seems that Spain's midfield options are boundless. As per usual, whoever is on the field, a high level of passing will commence.

Spain is just too good, too organized, and too much to handle for most sides...good luck if you're going up against the Spaniards; it will probably be a bad experience, the kind where you never touch the ball, and, if you do, if you're only so lucky, you'll feel like it doesn't belong to you. It is likely that the only way to beat them will be a penalty shootout.

WHAT ARE THEIR CHANCES OF WINNING THE EURO THIS YEAR?

Very good—top of the list. Spain is just too talented. Watch out for a possible championship run. Though, for what it's worth, given that the Golden Generation has essentially dwindled away, I wouldn't be surprised if this isn't Spain's year. Also, for the same reason, Spain probably won't win the 2024 or 2028 Euros either. Will it take Spain 36 years to win its next UEFA Euro? Nobody knows for sure. But one thing is certain. Spain will always be a world leader. However, without the right chemistry of talent it will just be a supremely talented group of players going through the motions of highly technical, well-orchestrated tactical soccer played at a PhD level. It will need a special generation to emerge—with a unique will to win—in order to reignite the success from 2008 to 2012.

SWITZERLAND

Euro Cup: 0
World Cup: 0
Overall Team Rating: 7.7

Known For
Josef Hügi
Heinz Hermann
Alexander Frei
Granit Xhaka
Xherdan Shaqiri
Haris Seferović

A BRIEF TEAM HISTORY

Switzerland's UEFA Euro adventure. Where do we start? Well, how about the beginning?

From 1960-1992, Switzerland didn't compete in a UEFA Euro. Ouch. Brutal. That's a rough start.

Then in 1996 things changed. Not only did Switzerland qualify, finally, but it didn't get out of its group. Oy vey. Well, we weren't expecting the world to change, quite yet.

UEFA Euro 2000 was back to the basics—Switzerland didn't compete. Then came 2004 and 2008 (come on, Switzerland, you can do it!), and without fail, despite participating, the Swiss couldn't get past the group stage. In 2012, Switzerland was like, "Hold on. We're getting ahead of ourselves. Let's not qualify again." And it didn't. Most recently, in 2016, Switzerland had its best Euro performance yet as it made the Round of 16. And that was it.

It has been a Euro history not of "trophies" and "accolades," but of "average" (if not below average) and "disappointment." Though the Swiss feel like it's a time for change. Switzerland is a nation ready to seize the grand stage of international soccer, starting with UEFA Euro 2020. Will the Swiss do it? That is, will the Swiss walk away with the championship trophy, thus astonishing everyone in Europe and around the world in the process? Probably not. In fact, probably not is code for don't get your hopes up, which is code for absolutely not. But there is a chance, however, we are leaning toward no. By we, I mean pretty much everyone in the world, Europe, and even Switzerland.

However, Switzerland is back, ready for action, ready to improve.

FACTS ABOUT THEIR COUNTRY

Switzerland, a small Central European nation, is a beautiful tourist destination known for mountains, skiing, clocks, and banks. When it comes to banks, Switzerland takes the handling of money very seriously. Patrick Radden Keefe, whose story appeared in *The New Yorker*, wrote: "Since 1713, when the Great Council of Geneva banned banks from revealing the private information of their customers, Switzerland had thrived on its reputation as a stronghold of financial secrecy. International élites could place their fortunes beyond the reach of tax authorities in their own countries."[13]

In the world of sports, Switzerland is known for tennis great, Roger Federer. When it comes to soccer, Switzerland has always been a competitive team but it is one that is looking for a major tournament championship.

A few beers that may be passed around as fans watch the games include Erdinger and Vollmond.

WHERE THE TEAM IS TODAY—
TACTICS AND STRATEGIES

Switzerland has a big challenge on its hands. It's not a team that has caused concern for opponents. Well, that's not completely true. Teams are always weary of Switzerland but not completely afraid. It has proven to be an average program over the generations with moments of greatness. In fact, in World Cup 2010, Switzerland pulled off a major upset by defeating the eventual champions, Spain, in the group stage. In general, little is expected from the Swiss. So how can Switzerland change its course? How can it get things going toward a championship?

Tactics and strategies: Adopt a Spanish approach to the game. Look, Switzerland isn't known for flashy play. It's a pretty straightforward team, one that has constructive passing and decent organization on both sides of the ball. It is a boring team, let's be honest. It has athletes but no game-changers. Frankly, there are no Messi-types lurking around. So why not go with the Spanish approach? By this, I mean completely go for domination in possession soccer and by keeping the ball away from the opposition the Swiss can improve on scoring chances in the long run. Otherwise, if it trades punches with opponents, then it is really just playing into the hands of history, which has shown the Swiss to be nothing more than a good sparring partner. Instead, own possession, own the game, and see what happens.

On its quest for European greatness, Switzerland will likely go with a 3-5-2 or maybe a 4-3-3. We shall see. Formations can change yet Switzerland's attention to detail in terms of possession will be very important if it wants to potentially win the tournament. Because without possession on Switzerland's side, it is not going to win this tournament by trading punches with other top teams. Perhaps, if the Swiss stick to a strong game plan as just laid out, the headlines will read: "Switzerland, Kings of Europe! The Swiss take its first Euro Cup in amazing fashion!" Well, maybe not. Look, it will be a stringent challenge for Switzerland to conquer the continent. It just might take a little time.

VLADIMIR PETKOVI —A BRIEF COACHING PORTRAIT

Vladimir Petković, who was born in 1963, has been coaching Switzerland for about six years now. It should go without saying, he's got a massive challenge on his hands. That challenge is to get Switzerland a championship or past the Round of 16. The latter is the best Switzerland has done in the UEFA Euro. The former would be an outright dream come true for Swiss fans everywhere. Should Petković pull it off, he would be a legend beyond legend in the mountainous land known as Switzerland.

KEY PLAYERS AND THEIR CHARACTERISTICS

Granit Xhaka, Xherdan Shaqiri, and Haris Seferović

Granit Xhaka played over 100 games with Borussia Monchen-gladbach before joining Arsenal where he has done well as a midfielder. He was born in 1992 in Switzerland, and winning the UEFA Euro would be an earth-changing achievement for him and the team. As one of the leaders, he is expected to bring in all his experience from the EPL to put his side over the top.

Xherdan Shaqiri, who was born in Yugoslavia in 1991, is an outside player that will push the tempo with runs down the wing. The experienced player with Liverpool will be counted on for guidance, defense out wide, surging runs, and goals throughout the tournament.

Haris Seferović—a Swiss forward—is ready to round up a number of goals. He joined Benfica in 2017 and has done well with goals (over 25 and counting). Is he Romario, Timo Werner, or Messi? No, no, and hell no. So how much can he offer? Fans of Switzerland will be looking for Seferović to be creative up top and put in some goals for sure. However, if he's not scoring he'll have to be productive with passing and getting others involved.

Overall Player Rating:
Granit Xhaka: 9
Xherdan Shaqiri: 7.9
Haris Seferović: 8.9

KEY PLAYER STATS

(Total career goals for their country)

	Games Played	Goals
Granit Xhaka	82	12
Xherdan Shaqiri	82	22
Haris Seferović	64	18

WHAT TO WATCH FOR ON TV—HOW MBAPPÉ, RONALDO, AND OTHERS PLAY

The Swiss have a goal and that is to advance further than the Round of 16. Then, if all plays out according to plan, it would hope for an actual championship. What might help the Swiss achieve this goal? Hmmm, pretty easy: Get Neymar Swiss citizenship. The problem with Switzerland is that it lacks real game-changers, such as Neymar, Messi, or Cristiano Ronaldo. There's not much depth in the dribble, is there? It's a team that needs individual playmakers with ingenuity, creativity, and, as Steve McManaman might say, guile.

You can invest your money in their banks, but maybe not their players. Again, the players are solid, competitive, talented... but not quite as solid, competitive, or talented as a team like Germany or Spain. It's a team that lacks creativity and a will to win on the biggest stage.

This is a team that can bore the living daylights out of you (1954-2010) or come up with a massive upset (Spain, World Cup 2010). Either way, you're not chatting at the concession stand about that amazing game Switzerland just had, unless, of course, we're talking about the 1-0 2010 upset over the soon-to-be champs. But hold on. Timeout. This big upset over Spain in 2010 was not what it seems. On paper it seems great. Switzerland won! Yeah, a little deceiving. If you actually watched the game, with a critical eye, combined with a tiny amount of common sense, you would know that Spain completely outplayed the Swiss and the Central European underdogs managed to sneak in a lucky goal and held on for dear life. But, without a doubt, some 10 years later, it's 2020 and there's hope for the Swiss in this competition. Not much hope, but it's there. There's a chance that this small nation—who doesn't have a record to stand on, who doesn't have star players, who doesn't have any realistic chance to win the Euro Cup—will surpass all odds and walk away as the number one team in Europe. There is always hope. But I wouldn't bet the bank on it, Swiss or otherwise.

WHAT ARE THEIR CHANCES OF WINNING THE EURO THIS YEAR?

Not so good—bottom of the list.

DENMARK

Euro Cup: 1
World Cup: 0
Overall Team Rating: 8.6

Known For
Passionate fans
The 1992 UEFA Euro Championship
An exciting 1986 World Cup
Solid teams
Preben Elkjaer
Michael Laudrup
Simon Kjaer
Christian Eriksen

A BRIEF TEAM HISTORY

Founded in 1889, Danish soccer has a long history within Europe. As for the UEFA Euro, Denmark has experienced an interesting journey.

In 1960, Denmark didn't compete in the first UEFA Euro.

In 1964, Denmark competed and placed fourth. A pretty good result.

Then from 1968 to 1980, Denmark didn't compete in the Euro. What happened? Apparently Denmark was hibernating.

In 1984, after a long absence, Denmark made the semi-finals. Not bad.

In 1988, it couldn't get out of its group.

The big year for the Danes arrived in 1992. Up to this point, it seemed as though "not so great" in the Euro was becoming so passé that Denmark wanted to take a stand. And take a stand it did. No one expected it, but, against all odds, Denmark won the UEFA Euro this year. It was a phenomenal result. A mega-accomplishment. The world took notice. Denmark had done it. It stormed the castle of Europe and took no prisoners.

Since 1992, I guess you could say things went back to normal for the Danes. That is, if you consider normal to be absolutely average.

In 1996, Denmark didn't get out of its group. As for 2000, the same occurred. Things improved in 2004 as Denmark made it to the quarter-finals. In 2008, things took a turn for the worse as Denmark didn't compete.

In 2012, Denmark participated but couldn't get out of its group. In 2016, it was back to the drawing board, as Denmark didn't compete. As for 2020, the Danes are back and ready to relive 1992 all over again. That's the plan anyway.

FACTS ABOUT THEIR COUNTRY

Denmark might be known for Shakespearean tragedy and amazing castles but it is also internationally regarded for beer. During the 2020 UEFA Euro, many Danes will enjoy a wide selection of domestic beers, including Albani Giraf Gold and Carls Porter.

Soccer reigns supreme in Denmark. The leading scorer in Denmark's history is Jon Dahl Tomasson (1997-2010), with 52.

WHERE THE TEAM IS TODAY— TACTICS AND STRATEGIES

Denmark has a talented team as usual. But can it live up to championship status?

Tactics and strategies: Defense and short-passing.

The Danes stand strong on defense, and, in terms of offense, it is a team that excels at short-passing. Its approach offensively is often patient. It is a smart team that exudes skill. In essence, its style would be a combination of Germany and Netherlands.

Denmark has always had top talent but has had a tough time bringing everything together on the World Cup stage. On the other hand, in 1992, the Danes brought home the UEFA Euro trophy, its biggest achievement to date. It hopes to regain the title in 2020 and on route to this goal the Danes will likely field a 4-2-3-1.

Can you count on Denmark to win it all, again? No, not really. But here's the thing with Denmark: They are always good. You never can truly tell if this will be the year or not. It could be. Then again, it probably won't. But ever since the dazzling Danes of 1986 and the castle-storming Danes of 1992, a special vibe rests with any Danish team; there's a feeling of potential greatness in the air. From the opponents' point of view, there is a feeling of latent trepidation. It will be difficult for Denmark to follow up its 1992 championship run, although this present team will do all it can to embody the will to win of that previous generation.

It will need to hold up defensively and block as many goals as possible. Easier said than done. The lower Denmark can keep the score, the better. Offensively, if Denmark can find a good flow in its possession game then many scoring chances should come its way. When many scoring chances arise, that's a good thing. Denmark has possession in its favor, which should only help its cause.

AGE HAREIDE—A BRIEF COACHING PORTRAIT

Age Hareide has been coaching Denmark since 2016. He didn't go too far. He is originally from Norway and played as a defender for his home country from 1976-1986. Don't be surprised to see a 3-5-2 formation. When Denmark is playing at its best, the ball is moving from side to side, and there is a flow established with frequent touches between players. You would think the two-man game aspect (emphasized by Spain) would be more prevalent, but it isn't. Will this be an issue moving forward? Possibly. You see, Denmark has the two-man game approach in its soccer DNA, and it is a matter of the coach seeing this possibility. (The two-man game establishes ultra-dominance in possession. Denmark could use this to its advantage. Without frequent use of the two-man game, Denmark may fizzle out in scoring situations.) Another problem is that Denmark doesn't have any true star power in the lineup. Good players, yes. The pride of Denmark, yes. But no out-and-out stars, such as Messi, Ronaldo, Salah, or Neymar. When you don't have stars, sometimes you don't have massive amounts of goals. This may hold the team back, and, frankly, it's an issue that's out of the coach's hands. Perhaps there are better lineup choices, which in fact would fall on the coach, but this seems like the best Denmark has to offer. The world will have to wait and see. Regardless, under Hareide's direction, the team has a thoughtful approach, relying on skill reminiscent from indoor soccer to get scoring chances. Over the long duration of a tournament, this should serve the Danes well.

KEY PLAYERS AND THEIR CHARACTERISTICS

Simon Kjaer and Christian Eriksen

Simon Kjaer is a lively, energetic, and passionate player more than willing to dish out a hard tackle. The center defender was born in Horsens, Denmark, and has experience playing for Roma and Lille. His time with these high-quality clubs should help guide Denmark forward. A lot is riding on this tournament for Denmark, and Kjaer will be pivotal for success.

Christian Eriksen was born in 1992, which is interesting as this was the year Denmark won its only Euro Cup. He's a versatile midfielder, equipped with indoor skill. He did well with Ajax (25 goals), and signed with Tottenham in 2013. All of his vast experience from the EPL should be an asset for Denmark throughout the tournament. He is a consistent scorer and Denmark is one step closer to the title with him on the field.

Overall Player Rating:
Simon Kjaer: 9.1
Christian Eriksen: 9.1

KEY PLAYER STATS

(Total career goals for their country)

	Games Played	Goals
Simon Kjaer	97	3
Christian Eriksen	95	31

WHAT TO WATCH FOR ON TV—HOW MBAPPÉ, RONALDO, AND OTHERS PLAY

Simon Kjaer and Christian Eriksen will be guiding the team forward. Other important pieces include Nicolai Jørgensen and Yussuf Poulsen; these are two talented scorers sure to be around the goal; with them up top, Denmark is within reach of a run for the title.

Probably operating out of a 4-2-3-1, Denmark will throw a lot of short passes at opponents and keep them off-balance along the way.

Backed by a strong defense, the Danes will be a tough team to deal with all tournament long. Will its keeper need to make 54 saves in order to remain viable? Well, that might be asking a lot but Denmark should have a strong enough defense to keep scores low.

Don't be surprised to see a good run from Denmark, a team on a quest to reunite with the 1992 title some 28 years later.

WHAT ARE THEIR CHANCES OF WINNING THE EURO THIS YEAR?

Pretty good, but not great. Denmark lies somewhere in the middle of the list.

RUSSIA

Euro Cup: 1
World Cup: 0
Overall Team Rating: 8.8-9

Known For
Very passionate fans
A history of good teams
One UEFA Euro championship as the Soviet Union
Yuri Zhirkov
Artem Dzyuba
Fedor (Fyodor) Chalov

A QUICK GLANCE

Russia, part of the former Soviet Union, won the first UEFA Euro
back in 1960. It was an era when the Soviet Union was a force to
be reckoned with in practically all sports. Hockey and gymnastics
were top of the list for Soviet achievements. (Let's not forget
chess. It's not a sport in the traditional sense; however, the Soviet
Union and Russia have had a major impact in the competitive
world of chess, a game that has practical learning applications for
sports such as soccer.) Soccer was up there as well. In fact, as for

the UEFA Euro, Russia has had a very eventful run. (Keep in mind, we are including the former Soviet Union here along with Russia.)

The UEFA Euro of 1960 was a grand accomplishment for the Soviet Union. For the opening tournament, the Soviets took home first place.

Then in 1964, the Soviets did very well and placed second.

As for 1968, the Soviet Union placed fourth.

In 1972, the Soviets came up big again and placed second.

As for 1976, 1980, and 1984, things slowed down a little bit on the soccer front as the Soviets didn't compete in the UEFA Euro.

The Euro of 1988 was a strong showing for the USSR. Things got back to normal as the Soviets eventually placed second.

In 1992, competing as CIS, the team didn't advance out of its group.

In 1996, competing as Russia for the first time in a UEFA Euro, the team could not get out of its group.

In 2000, the Russians didn't qualify.

As for 2004, Russia was back in the UEFA Euro but couldn't get out of its group.

In 2008, things improved greatly as Russia reached the semi-finals.

In 2012 and 2016, Russia competed in the UEFA Euro but couldn't get past its group.

As for 2020, the Russians are looking to have a statement year. Don't be surprised to see a 4-2-3-1 on route to a great tournament.

Tactics and strategies: Russia, a country with so much talent, needs to work on its consistency around goal and on defense. There is no reason that Russia can't find its way into the semi-finals. If it can stay consistent on both sides of the ball, good things can happen. And, what's of equal importance is that if the Russians can isolate long stints of possession, a big improvement in major tournaments should follow. Russia will dabble in possession but once it really owns it, then things could possibly shift in a big way. After all, possession soccer is highly suited for Russians. Possession soccer is a thinking man's game and who better to outthink someone than the Russians? Anyone heard of chess? The Russians certainly have. Russians are the equivalent of Brazilian soccer players in the world of chess. Therefore, if Russia really commits to owning possession soccer—which means taking over the ball with no intent of giving it up, similar to Spain—then other teams will begin to suffer more losses at the hands of the world's largest geographic country.

KEY PLAYERS AND THEIR CHARACTERISTICS

Artem Dzyuba and Fedor (Fyodor) Chalov

Artem Dzyuba is a forward that joined Zenit Saint Petersburg in 2015. He is a taller player that can cause trouble in the box with crosses. His strong presence up top will be a handful for opposing defenses.

Fedor Chalov is a standout scorer for CSKA Moscow. He is also an able assist provider. He was born in 1998 and the youngster has a chance to win Russia a UEFA Euro championship early in his career. He's an up and coming talent for Russia, one to keep an eye on, as he might be one of the nation's next big stars.

Overall Player Rating:
Artem Dzyuba: 8.8
Fedor Chalov: 9

KEY PLAYER STATS

(Total career goals for their country)

	Games Played	Goals
Artem Dzyuba	42	24
Fedor Chalov	2	0

WHAT ARE THEIR CHANCES OF WINNING THE EURO THIS YEAR?

Not great, but it is possible. Russia's soccer program, which dates back to 1912, has a great opportunity to gather a first place trophy in 2020. It should be a great challenge but is definitely a goal within reach.

Euro Cup: 0
World Cup: 0
Overall Team Rating: 8

Known For
Quality soccer
Andriy Shevchenko

A QUICK GLANCE

Originally, Ukraine was under the umbrella of the Soviet Union. So from 1960-1992, Ukraine didn't compete in the UEFA Euro.

From 1996 to 2008, Ukraine didn't make it to the big tournament.

Finally, in 2012, Ukraine qualified but couldn't escape its group.

The same occurred in 2016.

Could the UEFA Euro of 2020 be Ukraine's big year? Will it surpass all expectations, which are low, and win the whole thing? It's possible but highly unlikely. That's not to say that Ukraine is no good. Quite the opposite. Ukraine is almost always a viable opponent for any side in the world.

You will likely see Ukraine in a 4-3-3. On its quest to winning UEFA Euro 2020, or at least reaching the quarter-finals, Ukraine has a great opportunity to make a big splash this tournament. Maybe, just maybe, it will pull off a miracle.

Tactics and strategies: Stay on course defensively, concentrate on possession, and keep the flow of play simple. Anything too complicated in the strategy department might disrupt the flow of play for Ukraine. Concentrating on possession will be the best option for success. If possession is front and center for Ukraine, then quality scoring chances will be around the corner.

KEY PLAYERS AND THEIR CHARACTERISTICS

Andriy Yarmolenko and Yevhen Olehovych Konoplyanka

Andriy Yarmolenko—born in 1989—is an attacking player to watch out for this tournament. He racked up a ton of goals (99) during his time at Dynamo Kyiv and also brings in experience from Borussia Dortmund and West Ham. Ukraine is hoping to lean on his talent for a good chance at winning UEFA Euro 2020.

Yevhen Olehovych Konoplyanka—referred to as Yevhen Konoplyanka—has played with Ukraine since 2010. Now, with around 10 years of experience at the top level of his country, this might be the last chance for him to capture a UEFA Euro title. The pressure is on. He will be expected to deliver big-time in order for Ukraine to achieve the ultimate European championship.

Overall Player Rating:
Andriy Yarmolenko: 9
Yevhen Konoplyanka: 9

KEY PLAYER STATS

(Total career goals for their country)

	Games Played	Goals
Andriy Yarmolenko	83	37
Yevhen Konoplyanka	85	21

WHAT ARE THEIR CHANCES OF WINNING THE EURO THIS YEAR?

You never know.

CROATIA

Euro Cup: 0
World Cup: 0
Overall Team Rating: 9-9.3

Known For
Placing second in the 2018 World Cup
Strong attendance
Very passionate fans
Exciting games
High-quality football
Zvonimir Boban
Luka Modrić
Ivan Rakitić
Ivan Perišić

A QUICK GLANCE

Croatia has been doing very well of late. As everyone knows,
or should know, Croatia placed second in the 2018 FIFA World
Cup, as it lost to France in the final. The Croatians had a great
tournament that year and came so close to winning the grand
prize. Now Croatia has its eyes set on the UEFA Euro. With

talent like Luka Modrić and Ivan Rakitić, nothing is out of reach but Croatia doesn't have the best track record when it comes to previous UEFA Euro tournaments.

From 1960 to 1992, Croatia was under the umbrella of Yugoslavia. In 1996, Croatia made the quarter-finals of the UEFA Euro which was held in England that year. As for the Euro of 2000, Croatia didn't make the big dance.

In 2004, Croatia made the big tournament but it couldn't escape its group. The Euro of 2008 would be different as Croatia made the quarter-finals. In 2012, things got less exciting for Croatia. It made the tournament but couldn't escape its group. Croatia had a much better result in the 2016 Euro as it reached the Round of 16. This was followed up by an astounding result at the aforementioned 2018 FIFA World Cup in which Croatia earned second-place overall.

Luka Modrić—Croatia's leading star player—has a ton of success from Real Madrid, not to mention a Ballon d'Or. As for the latter, Modrić broke the long streak of the award going back-and-forth between Messi and Cristiano Ronaldo. With Modrić playing at a top level, distributing the ball with an artistic touch of brilliance, Croatia has a great chance of shaking things up in the 2020 UEFA Euro.

Tactics and strategies: Get the ball to the feet of Luka Modrić, Ivan Rakitić, and Ivan Perišić as much as possible. These players are responsible for establishing a flow to the game. Of course, without a doubt, it should go without saying but needs to be said nonetheless, the support players will play a valuable role throughout the duration of a game and the tournament at large. However, having said that, the three players previously mentioned are the generals, and the creative pulse beats through them.

Formations can always change, you never know. Having said that, watch for a 4-2-3-1 as Croatia moves throughout the tournament. Also, Croatia has very passionate fans. They really seem to support their players, especially Perišić.

KEY PLAYERS AND THEIR CHARACTERISTICS

Luka Modrić, Ivan Rakitić, and Ivan Perišić

Luka Modrić has the world on a string with his passing, field vision, field organization, and accomplishments. Along with winning the Champions League with Real Madrid, he earned a second-place finish in the 2018 FIFA World Cup, with a little-known trophy called the Ballon d'Or tucked away as well. It would be truly remarkable for Modrić and Croatia to win the 2020 UEFA Euro, which is highly possible with one of the best midfielders in the world at the helm. Some players pass the ball well. You can see it in their technique, and how the ball moves. Modrić, in this regard, is top of the list.

Ivan Rakitić is right there with Modrić as a passing expert. He and Modrić make a formidable combination for any team to deal with. On top of this, his experience from Barcelona, one of the world's elite passing clubs, will definitely serve Croatia well on its quest for the 2020 UEFA Euro. With Rakitić serving up well-designed passes from midfield, this is a goal that is completely within reach.

Ivan Perišić is like the front man and recipient of all the greatness provided in the midfield from Modrić and Rakitić. He adds a dynamic presence up top and out wide with dribbling, bursts of speed, and a willingness to find areas behind vulnerable defenses.

Overall Player Rating:
Luka Modrić: 9.8
Ivan Rakitić: 9.3
Ivan Perišić: 9.2

KEY PLAYER STATS

(Total career goals for their country)

	Games Played	Goals
Luka Modrić	127	16
Ivan Rakitić	106	15
Ivan Perišić	88	26

WHAT ARE THEIR CHANCES OF WINNING THE EURO THIS YEAR?

Croatia's chances of winning are not super low. In fact, if a smaller nation should win this year, it might in fact be Croatia.

SWEDEN

Euro Cup: 0
World Cup: 0
Overall Team Rating: 7.8-8

Known For
Strong attendance
Very passionate fans
Long history of football
Good talent
Zlatan Ibrahimović

A QUICK GLANCE

Where do we start with Sweden? It's such a good soccer-producing country yet has never really gotten a big result. This is especially true when it comes to the UEFA Euro.

Sweden's record in Europe's biggest tournament? Not great.

From 1960-1988, Sweden didn't compete. Not a great start. However, lo and behold, in 1992, during Sweden's first appearance in the Euro, it got to the semi-finals and placed third overall. Pretty good. In 1996, Sweden didn't compete, yet again.

As for 2000, Sweden couldn't escape its group. In 2004, Sweden made the quarter-finals. Then in 2008, 2012, and 2016, Sweden was a contender but couldn't escape its group. Will UEFA Euro 2020 bring a whole lot of average for Sweden? Unfortunately, based on its record: Yes.

Tactics and strategies: Given that Sweden doesn't have outright super-star talent, it should concentrate on solid performances across the board from each player with an eye on steady, unified defense, coupled with a simple buildup in possession. Sweden will probably operate out of a 4-4-2. A simple buildup in possession should ease the nerves of the players, who, grant it, are experienced and talented professionals, yet while Sweden is on the biggest stage, these players will feel the pressure. Furthermore, these players will feel the pressure based on the reality of Sweden's dismal and average track record in the Euro. The players know that winning the whole tournament is a far-fetched notion. However, a simple buildup in possession will be the only hope Sweden has to really make a push for the title. Don't overcomplicate things, keep ball movements simple, be patient around the box, avoid blind crosses, and good things should happen.

KEY PLAYERS AND THEIR CHARACTERISTICS

Sebastian Larsson, Marcus Berg, and Emil Forsberg

Sebastian Larsson brings to the table experience from Sunderland and Hull City, among other places. He's gathered over a 100 games for Sweden and his guidance up front will be crucial for Sweden's success in UEFA Euro 2020.

Marcus Berg—born in 1986—is a forward that will help Sweden get to the promise land, a UEFA Euro championship. He is a leading scorer for this Swedish team as he leaned on 20 goals for his country upon entering UEFA Euro 2020.

Emil Forsberg has over 125 games with RB Leipzig, and with Sweden has accumulated over 45 games. Forsberg—who can be found in the midfield—has a formidable shot from around the top of the box which could help Sweden during UEFA Euro 2020.

Overall Player Rating:
Sebastian Larsson: 8.8
Marcus Berg: 8.8
Emil Forsberg: 8.9

KEY PLAYER STATS

(Total career goals for their country)

	Games Played	**Goals**
Sebastian Larsson	118	8
Marcus Berg	76	21
Emil Forsberg	49	8

WHAT ARE THEIR CHANCES OF WINNING THE EURO THIS YEAR?

Sweden has a good team but is also one of the least likely teams to win the 2020 UEFA Euro.

POLAND

Euro Cup: 0
World Cup: 0
Overall Team Rating: 8.1-8.5

Known For
Strong attendance
Very passionate fans
Long history of football
Good teams from the 1970s and 80s
Robert Lewandowski

A QUICK GLANCE

Poland is always going to produce a strong team, one that can compete with any top talent around. However, like many other nations, Poland is still searching for that one major championship. To date, it has not yet won a UEFA Euro title. This will possibly be the year. Or perhaps it won't. As for past UEFA Euros, Poland has struggled to find its way a bit. Let's just say the UEFA Euro hasn't seen much of Poland over the years.

From 1960 through 2004, Poland didn't compete in a Euro. Wow...*wow*. In 2008 and 2012, Poland finally made the big dance but couldn't get out of its group. As for 2016, Poland got to the quarter-finals.

It should go without saying, UEFA Euro 2020 is a big deal for Poland and it's a country intent on making some progress for sure. Will it walk away with the championship trophy? Will Poland pull off a small miracle? Who knows at this point. Anything is possible and Poland is counting on a big performance from its players who will probably be lined up in a 4-4-2 or a 4-2-3-1.

Let's face it: On the way to UEFA Euro 2020, Poland had a very easy qualifying group. It consisted of Israel (not a threat), North Macedonia (we'll get to them in a second), Slovenia (not the best team in the world), Austria (ehhhh x 10), and Latvia (forget about it). I mean, give me a break. Seriously? Poland could only be so lucky. Who even knew North Macedonia had a team? Well, with a little research it is true, not only does it have a soccer team, but it was in Poland's UEFA Euro 2020 qualifying group. And, oddly enough, one could argue that North Macedonia is a better soccer-playing nation than Latvia. That aside, here's the deal: Poland might just have a rude awakening when it enters UEFA Euro 2020 and takes a flurry of punches from top-tier opponents.

Tactics and strategies: Realistically, Poland should get the ball to Robert Lewandowski as much as possible. Frankly, this is Poland's only hope. But this raises an interesting question. Is this the best strategy? After all, Lewandowski is a goal-scorer for the ages. But if you only concentrate on getting the ball to one player, then a reverse effect of negative soccer tends to follow.

A one-trick pony is never a good thing to be as a team. When everyone starts buying into the idea that getting the ball to one player is the best option for success, then other positions will be neglected and the overall style of the team will suffer. Not to mention, the approach will be very predictable. As much as Poland can get things going for Lewandowski, it should also get others involved in a big way. If everyone is clicking then good things will be around the corner.

KEY PLAYERS AND THEIR CHARACTERISTICS

Robert Lewandowski, Jakub Błaszczykowski, and Arkadiusz Milik

Robert Lewandowski is arguably Poland's best player of all time. He is definitely one of the world's elite scoring forces at the moment. Whether it's with Bayern Munich or Poland, he threatens to score during any game with classical finishing technique and is always a game-changing presence up top.

Jakub Błaszczykowski—who is known in some circles as "the easiest last name to spell"—was born in 1985 and has playing experience at Borussia Dortmund, among other places. He can be found on the outside where he will be representing Poland on its quest to get Robert Lewandowski the ball in strong scoring positions. Jakub should likely help in this regard as Poland sets out to conquer UEFA Euro 2020.

Arkadiusz Milik—who was born in 1994 in Poland—is a forward with over 70 games played and 33 goals scored with Napoli to date. Considering his experience in Serie A, he should likely be a strong force within Poland's lineup during UEFA Euro 2020.

Overall Player Rating:
Robert Lewandowski: 9.5
Jakub Błaszczykowski: 8.8
Arkadiusz Milik: 8.3

KEY PLAYER STATS

(Total career goals for their country)

	Games Played	Goals
Robert Lewandowski	112	61
Jakub Błaszczykowski	108	21
Arkadiusz Milik	49	14

WHAT ARE THEIR CHANCES OF WINNING THE EURO THIS YEAR?

Not the best.

AUSTRIA

Euro Cup: 0
World Cup: 0
Overall Team Rating: 7.6-7.8

Known For
Good teams
Passionate fans
A team searching for a major tournament championship
Matthias Sindelar

A QUICK GLANCE

Austria is still searching for that one illusive major tournament championship. Will it get one? Will it finally step up to the winner's circle? By the looks of it, this might not be the year. Judging by past UEFA Euros, this definitely will not be the year.

From 1960 to 2004, Austria didn't compete. Not the best start.

In 2008, Austria made its first appearance in a UEFA Euro tournament. Finally. Many years had passed, and it finally made the big dance. However, Austria had to make an early exit because it couldn't advance out of its group. Better luck next time.

That next time, in fact, turned out to take a while.

In 2012, Austria didn't make the tournament.

Then in 2016, Austria qualified for the second time in its history, but yet again, it couldn't get beyond the group stage.

Having said that, Austria has its sights on making this 2020 UEFA Euro a memorable year. In fact, from Austria's point of view, what better time to win than right now? You never know. Austria could do it. It could pull off a miracle and walk away as the number one team in Europe. Just as Denmark did in 1992. Just as Greece did in 2004. It's highly unlikely, but possible.

Tactics and strategies: Don't get swept up by better teams having the majority of possession. Play your game, keep the passing combinations simple yet consistent and good things should follow.

Austria will probably take its chances with a 4-2-3-1.

KEY PLAYERS AND THEIR CHARACTERISTICS

Marko Arnautović, Marcel Sabitzer, Julian Baumgartlinger, and Valentino Lazaro

Marko Arnautović is a forward that Austria leans on for goals, plain and simple. He might not be a household name but he's a reliable scoring threat for his national team. In fact, Austria has a pretty low-scoring team, and he leads the pack. With this comes a lot of pressure. He will be counted on for the lion's share of scoring and such a responsibility can be a burden. When a team relies on one player for scoring too much, it can have a negative effect. It becomes predictable for defenses and someone like Marko is stuck with extra coverage which can lead to fewer goals. So a challenge for Austria will be to get Marko touches on the ball with the idea of *just getting touches on the ball* while also getting other teammates involved around goal. As a result, good things should be around the corner. The paradox is the following: If Marko only tries to score, it probably won't happen. But if he can get simple touches on the ball (away from goal), then a positive progressive buildup should theoretically occur.

Marcel Sabitzer is an attacking player with over 130 games with RB Leipzig, one of the most protested teams in Europe. He's scored a number of goals in his club career, though with over 40 caps for Austria, he has only placed seven in the back of the net (as of January 2020). It's not the worst in the world, but it could use improvement. Austrian fans are hoping he can knock in a few during UEFA Euro 2020. What's also important will be his ability to get assists and contribute in possession play for his team to have good scoring opportunities.

Julian Baumgartlinger, Austria's captain, is a midfielder that plays club ball with Bayern Leverkusen. To say he scores often would be completely misleading. While he is likely not going to put the ball in the back of the net (he only had one goal in 74 games for his country), his leadership is what Austria is counting on for optimum success in UEFA Euro 2020.

Valentino Lazaro is an outside midfielder that has a small amount of goals with Austria. Though he's playing a role that consists of keeping the flow of play going offensively while holding up opposition attacks defensively.

Overall Player Rating:
Marko Arnautović: 8.9
Marcel Sabitzer: 8.9
Julian Baumgartlinger: 8.7
Valentino Lazaro: 8.7

KEY PLAYER STATS

(Total career goals for their country)

	Games Played	Goals
Marko Arnautović	85	26
Marcel Sabitzer	42	7
Julian Baumgartlinger	74	1
Valentino Lazaro	28	3

WHAT ARE THEIR CHANCES OF WINNING THE EURO THIS YEAR?

Not so great. In fact, don't bet the bank on it. I take that back. Don't bet *five dollars* on it.

TURKEY

Euro Cup: 0
World Cup: 0
Overall Team Rating: 8.5-8.9

Known For
Passionate fans
A program searching for a major tournament championship

A QUICK GLANCE

Turkey. Outside of making the semi-finals in the 2002 FIFA World Cup (in which it lost 1-0 to Brazil), Turkey hasn't made much of a splash in big tournaments. Let's take a look at the UEFA Euro, shall we? It won't be long, I can assure you that.

From 1960 to 1992, Turkey didn't compete. (What did I tell you?) Then, finally, in 1996, Turkey made the big show; it competed in the UEFA Euro. However, it couldn't get out of its group. Not much of a surprise, but, hey, if you're Turkey, what are you gonna do?

In 2000, Turkey improved substantially and made the quarter-finals. This was a big deal and a huge progression for Turkey. However, in 2004, Turkey didn't compete again. Lo and behold, in 2008, Turkey was back and made the semi-finals, its best result to date. In 2012, it didn't compete. In 2016, it couldn't get out of its group.

Turkey is counting on 2020 to be a big year. For the most part, Turkey has shown that it can exit a tournament very early and make the semi-finals. The latter is something to lean on. Sometimes, top teams (even Italy and Germany) can exit a tournament early. So to have reached the semi-finals is a confidence builder for Turkey, even if it is fielding a new group of players. It's a confidence that transcends to new generations.

Tactics and strategies: Generate some flow on offense. This is Turkey's only chance at greatness. It must take chances offensively and go for it.

Turkey might field a 4-2-3-1. But wait, there's more. Turkey might go with a 4-1-4-1, a formation it was using leading into UEFA Euro 2020. Will we see Turkey in a 4-4-2? It's possible. It used this formation as well. The 4-4-2 is a simple formation, one that might be of great use for Turkey in a high-stakes tournament like UEFA Euro 2020. All in all, Turkey should focus on one formation so its players don't get confused.

KEY PLAYERS AND THEIR CHARACTERISTICS

Emre Belözoğlu, Hakan Çalhanoğlu, Burak Yılmaz, and Cenk Tosun

Emre Belözoğlu—Turkey's captain and midfielder—brings a lot of professional experience from Inter Milan and Newcastle United, along with a few other places. He's going to be a presence for Turkey throughout the tournament. To date, he has hit the 100 game mark for his country.

Hakan Çalhanoğlu, who can be found professionally at AC Milan, is a game-changer. He's a fast forward that can make things happen quickly. Watch out for him as the tournament moves on.

Burak Yılmaz is a scorer. Keep an eye on him throughout the tournament as he can simply put the ball in the back of the net. To date, he has acquired 24 goals for his country and though he's getting older in soccer years, there are still plenty of opportunities around the corner.

Cenk Tosun has been gathering up games and goals for Everton in the EPL. The forward is hoping to produce for Turkey during UEFA Euro 2020. He's part of a talented team that could surprise many with a strong run this tournament. His production up top, combining passes with shots on goal, will be crucial for Turkey's potential success.

Overall Player Rating:
Emre Belözoğlu: 8.9
Hakan Çalhanoğlu: 9
Burak Yılmaz: 9
Cenk Tosun: 9

KEY PLAYER STATS

(Total career goals for their country)

	Games Played	Goals
Emre Belözoğlu	101	9
Hakan Çalhanoğlu	48	10
Burak Yılmaz	59	24
Cenk Tosun	42	16

WHAT ARE THEIR CHANCES OF WINNING THE EURO THIS YEAR?

Not great. Don't count on it. However, hold your horses. Turkey is full of surprises. Don't rule this team out completely. Turkey had a strong qualifying campaign and even defeated France—the current World Cup champs—2-0 in the process. Turkey is a team with a lot of pride; it is also a team with big plans. Here's the downside: To date, Turkey has not captured a major championship (a World Cup or UEFA Euro). So for Turkey to break through, it will take something very special. You never know, but you probably shouldn't bet the bank on Turkey.

CZECH REPUBLIC

Euro Cup: 1
World Cup: 0
Overall Team Rating: 8.1

Known For
Very passionate fans
Winning the 1976 Euro as Czechoslovakia

A QUICK GLANCE

Czech Republic is a team that can pull off a victory over a superior side on any given day. As Czechoslovakia, the team reached third place in 1960. For the tournaments of 1964, 1968, and 1972, it didn't compete. As for 1976, Czechoslovakia won the Euro, thus earning a major championship in the process. Since then, not much has happened in terms of winning a major tournament.

Though in 1980, it earned third place at the Euro. Then, for the Euro tournaments of 1984, 1988, and 1992, it didn't compete. In 1996, Czech Republic had a great result. It placed second overall, losing in the final to Germany.

In 2000, it qualified but couldn't escape its group. In 2004, it reached the semi-finals, a good result. In 2008, it couldn't escape its group. In 2012, it made the quarter-finals. In 2016, it couldn't escape its group. In fact, 1976 was the big moment, so far. The UEFA Euro of 2020 represents yet another opportunity for Czech Republic to gain prominence as a top-level team.

Tactics and strategies: Counterattack, and keep organized on defense. This will be Czech Republic's best chance to win the Euro again. This and a little luck...a lot of luck actually. Czech Republic will likely go with a 4-2-3-1 in an all-out attempt to take this tournament by storm.

KEY PLAYERS AND THEIR CHARACTERISTICS

Vladimír Darida, Michael Krmenčík, Patrik Schick, Alex Král, and Tomáš Souček

Born in 1990, **Vladimír Darida**, the team captain, is a midfielder ready to capture a championship. His team is gearing up for the ride of its life. He's been with the Czech Republic team since 2012 and one might think that a potential UEFA Euro title is now or never. Vladimír's downside: He isn't the biggest scorer. Vladimír's upside: Leadership and field organization are attributes he brings to the table. However it plays out, Vladimír should play a central role in Czech Republic's success.

Michael Krmenčík—born in 1993—is a 6'3" forward that has experience with Czech Republic since 2016. As of October 2019, when Czech Republic was still qualifying for UEFA Euro 2020,

Krmenčík had 8 goals in 19 games—a good goal to game ratio. He's one that Czech Republic should theoretically rely on for scoring, which will be of the utmost importance during this Euro competition.

Patrik Schick is a scorer. With experience from Roma, Sampdoria, and RB Leipzig, along with nine goals scored in 19 games for his country (as of January 2020), Schick is expected to bring home goals for Czech Republic during UEFA Euro 2020.

Alex Král is a midfielder that can guide things from the center of the field. Will he be able to take on the best of Europe and guide his team to a title? Tough call. Is he at the same level as Toni Kroos? Maybe not. Is he at the same level as Zinedine Zidane from years past? Definitely not. But he is a valuable asset right now for his country and fans are hoping that he brings home results.

Tomáš Souček is a midfielder that will hold things down for Czech Republic with defensive work and distributing the ball in transition. Is he a top-level midfielder that elite club teams are desperately recruiting? No. Is he something of a midfield savant? Not really. While he's not a household name, Souček is one that is going to do the work and hope for the best as his team looks to make history in UEFA Euro 2020.

Overall Player Rating:
Vladimír Darida: 9
Michael Krmenčík: 8.6
Patrik Schick: 9
Alex Král: 8.8
Tomáš Souček: 8.4

KEY PLAYER STATS

(Total career goals for their country)

	Games Played	Goals
Vladimír Darida	61	6
Michael Krmenčík	23	8
Patrik Schick	22	9
Alex Král	9	2
Tomáš Souček	25	3

WHAT ARE THEIR CHANCES OF WINNING THE EURO THIS YEAR?

Czech Republic has won the UEFA Euro before, though it was in 1976. It is a country that is always competitive, but I wouldn't count on a championship this time around. It's a team that lacks star power, excitement on offense, and depth from the bench. Without these things, Czech Republic just won't have enough in the tank to rank among the top teams. Unfortunately, for Czech Republic fans, there are just too many things holding the team back.

FINLAND

Euro Cup: 0
World Cup: 0
Overall Team Rating: 7

Known For
Passionate fans
A program on the rise searching for its first major championship

A QUICK GLANCE

Finland is one of those teams that will give a great effort and maybe win one over a superior opponent. The word "maybe" should be stressed. It is after all, Finland. It's just not a successful soccer-playing nation. That is just a fact. Should Finland win the 2020 UEFA Euro, media outlets around the world might collapse from too much activity. Arguably, it would be the story of the Century. But let's not get ahead of ourselves. There is no way Finland is going to win the 2020 UEFA Euro, or the next one or the one after that. We can keep going. But for now, let's realize how difficult it will be for Finland to win it all in 2020. Based on Finland's past record in the UEFA Euro, this is painfully obvious.

Let's put it this way: From 1960 to 2016, Finland didn't compete at all. Yes, you guessed it, this is Finland's very first UEFA Euro tournament! (And, this was probably my briefest team history ever. Thanks Finland!)

Tactics and strategies: While Finland will probably use a 4-4-2, it will need to possess the ball well, counterattack, keep scores low, and keep organized on defense. This will be Finland's best chance to win the Euro. Yet, it will have to do all these things extremely well. By extremely well, I mean something out of this world good. Though, realistically speaking, its best hope will be to somehow qualify for the elimination rounds. Let's be honest: This will be very difficult for Finland. It is an inexperienced nation at this tournament and it really has very little chance of success. To get out of its group, it will require a lot of luck, that's for sure. By a lot of luck, I mean that Finland will have to tie each game and pray that point differential goes in its favor. Then, should Finland be lucky enough to get into the elimination rounds, it will have to rally around the same strategy with this addendum: win every game in a penalty-kick shootout. There you go: Finland's path to the title.

KEY PLAYERS AND THEIR CHARACTERISTICS

Teemu Pukki, Robin Lod, and Glen Kamara

Teemu Pukki—a forward born in 1990—has experience with a number of clubs, some of which include Schalke 04, Celtic, and Norwich City. During his club stops, he has put in a number of goals, including 55 while he was with Brøndby IF in Denmark.

As for his time with Finland, Pukki has reached 25 goals and is looking for more. A great time to knock in a few more would be during UEFA Euro 2020, as fans from Finland will be counting on him for great results. Is he Paolo Rossi? No. Is he Marco van Basten? Nope. How about David Villa? Not quite. But he's got something, and that something helped to get Finland into the Euro for the first time; for this he deserves a lot of credit. As a result, Finland is betting the bank on his talents.

Robin Lod—born in 1993—is a midfielder typically found out wide. He currently plays with Minnesota United in Major League Soccer. Some say MLS is no man's land for international players in their prime. They say MLS is not worthy of European leagues. Well, that argument has persisted for many years now. However, as many know, MLS is gaining ground on all fronts and very soon it could—and theoretically should—be an elite world-class league. (Lod had been sharing his Minnesota United experience with a Finnish teammate, midfielder Rasmus Schüller. It will be interesting to see what role, if any, Schüller plays in UEFA Euro 2020.) Lod is currently capturing valuable playing experience from MLS. Essentially, he will need to be playing his best soccer for Finland to have a hope and a prayer during UEFA Euro 2020.

Glen Kamara is a midfielder with experience from Dundee and Rangers. As a driving force in Finland's lineup, he will need to be distributing the ball extremely efficiently during UEFA Euro 2020 to create chemistry with teammates. In doing so, if he can rally his team together with a few key assists here and there, then Finland might have a chance.

Overall Player Rating:
Teemu Pukki: 8.6
Robin Lod: 8.4
Glen Kamara: 8.6

KEY PLAYER STATS

(Total career goals for their country)

	Games Played	Goals
Teemu Pukki	80	25
Robin Lod	38	3
Glen Kamara	19	1

WHAT ARE THEIR CHANCES OF WINNING THE EURO THIS YEAR?

Let's put it this way: Finland's players might be fastidiously studying footage of Denmark 1992, Greece 2004, along with re-runs of *Hoosiers*. It won't help. It is a team that might, I stress, *might*, eventually pilfer a few goals here and there but nothing else. Finland's chances of winning the 2020 UEFA Euro are probably around zero. Correction: negative zero. A higher power would have to personally intervene for Finland to win this tournament. And this is nothing against Finland. It's just a fact that Finland is a massive underdog. Actually, for the next edition of *Webster's Dictionary*, for the word "underdog" you may as well forget about typing any definition with meddlesome words next to it and just place Finland's team photo. Will it take Finland 72 years to win a UEFA Euro championship? Maybe. Actually, it might take even longer.

WALES

Euro Cup: 0
World Cup: 0
Overall Team Rating: 7.9

Known For
A program searching for a major tournament championship
Ian Rush
Ryan Giggs
Gareth Bale
Aaron Ramsey

A QUICK GLANCE

Wales has a good team; however, as most people know, it's a group that will have to pull off a phenomenal tournament in order to walk away with the UEFA Euro 2020 first-place trophy. Prior to this tournament, the relationship between Wales and the UEFA Euro tournament has been close to non-existent. Let's take a look.

From 1960 to 2016, the only Euro Wales took part in was that of 2016 whereby it reached the semi-finals before losing to Portugal. Gareth Bale led the team with three goals that tournament. As you can see, UEFA Euro 2020 is only Wales's second attempt at European greatness. One step at a time. With only one previous Euro under its belt, Wales is currently in a place known as "better luck next time." It will be very difficult for Wales to repeat its accomplishment of reaching the semi-finals in 2020.

Tactics and strategies: Get the ball to Gareth Bale. After that, good luck. Probably operating out of a 4-2-3-1, Wales will likely lean on its star, Bale, for most of the attack. Aaron Ramsey, the recent Juventus signing, is available, along with others; however, when it comes down to it, Wales doesn't have much of a chance to win the 2020 UEFA Euro, so it might as well put all its eggs in one basket, that basket being Gareth Bale.

KEY PLAYERS AND THEIR CHARACTERISTICS

Gareth Bale and Aaron Ramsey

Gareth Bale is a dynamic force out wide with speed, agility, and an ability to get past defenders on route to goal where he's thundered in over 30 so far. His club career started with Southampton, then he signed with Tottenham, and eventually he landed with Real Madrid where he's become a leading force in La Liga. With Wales, he's seeking a big moment. Certainly, winning UEFA Euro 2020 would suffice. However, despite his talent, it will be difficult to earn a first-place finish.

Aaron Ramsey—born in 1990—is a versatile midfielder who has plenty of experience with Arsenal while also having earned some time with Cardiff City, Nottingham Forest, and most recently, Juventus. Ramsey should likely play a pivotal role in the attack for Wales, alongside Bale.

Overall Player Rating:
Gareth Bale: 9.3
Aaron Ramsey: 9

KEY PLAYER STATS

(Total career goals for their country)

	Games Played	Goals
Gareth Bale	83	33
Aaron Ramsey	60	16

WHAT ARE THEIR CHANCES OF WINNING THE EURO THIS YEAR?

We'll wait and see. By "wait and see," I mean we probably won't see them win. Though Wales should be very competitive.

****

These were the original 20 teams that qualified for the 24 openings in UEFA Euro 2020. As the UEFA Euro 2020 Qualification rounds wrapped up on November 19, 2019, the last four remaining slots were open. In March of 2020, after further qualifying competition, those four teams were determined. As is the nature of book publishing, this particular book had already been printed. So now is the chance for you to get involved! You can fill in those four teams right here, in the blanks provided.

Do any of these last-minute qualifiers have a chance to win UEFA Euro 2020? Anything's possible.

The 24 Teams of UEFA Euro 2020

France
England
Portugal
Germany
Netherlands
Belgium
Italy
Spain
Switzerland
Denmark
Russia
Ukraine
Croatia
Sweden
Poland
Austria
Turkey
Czech Republic
Finland
Wales
(The Last Four Teams to Qualify in March 2020.)

_____
_____
_____
_____

The Groups of UEFA Euro 2020

The following blank spaces are for the last four teams that qualified in March of 2020. This book was already published before then, so now is your chance to fill in those four teams right here.

Group A
Italy
Switzerland
Turkey
Wales

Group B
Belgium
Denmark
Finland
Russia

Group C
Austria
Netherlands

_____
Ukraine

Group D
Croatia
Czech Republic
England

_____

Group E

_____
Poland
Spain
Sweden

Group F
France
Germany

_____
Portugal

UEFA EURO CUP HISTORY: A BRIEF LOOK BACK

The monumental tournament for Europe's finest nations goes back to 1960, a year in which the first winner was a bit of a surprise. This isn't to say it was a complete surprise that the Soviet Union, a quality soccer-playing nation, set the tournament into motion with the first title. Since then, as you'll see, the top winners have been the Spanish and Germans, who each have three titles. The French are close behind with two titles.

Furthermore, Italy, a leader in World Cup titles, only has one UEFA Euro under its belt. Interestingly, you will probably notice, England does not have a UEFA Euro title. There are a few other surprises on this list as well. What surprises are yet to come in the years ahead? We will have to wait and see. Until now, it has been a very exciting journey.

Euro Winners Prior to 2020:
1960: Soviet Union
1964: Spain
1968: Italy
1972: West Germany
1976: Czechoslovakia
1980: West Germany
1984: France
1988: Netherlands
1992: Denmark
1996: Germany
2000: France
2004: Greece
2008: Spain
2012: Spain
2016: Portugal

1960: THE SOVIET UNION TAKES FIRST PRIZE

Once upon a time, in 1960, just two years after Pele and Garrincha led Brazil to its first World Cup title in Sweden, the Soviet Union might have caught some people off-guard by winning the first Euro Cup. But make no mistake, the Soviets were a devastatingly talented soccer-playing nation. So, was it such a surprise the Soviets won Euro 1960? Maybe a little bit but not so much. For the Soviets, the 1960 tournament played out like this: It was a brief affair. The tournament consisted of Czechoslovakia, the Soviet Union, France, and Yugoslavia. The games took place in France, Paris and Marseille to be exact. In the semi-finals, the Soviets took down Czechoslovakia 3-0. In the final, it stepped past Yugoslavia 2-1 with goals from Slava Metreveli and Viktor Ponedelnik. That was the first tournament, brief, succinct. Indeed times have changed.

1964: SPAIN WINS IT ALL

Spain hosted Euro 1964 and the home crowd proved to be on its side. Like the tournament of 1960, there were limited participants. In a straight semi-final format, Spain started out by defeating Hungary 2-1. The Soviet Union defeated Denmark in the other semi-final. In the final—which took place in one of Spain's treasured stadiums, the beautiful, exotic, and timeless Santiago Bernabéu in Madrid—Spain bested the Soviet Union by a score of 2-1, with goals from Jesús María Pereda and Marcelino Martínez. It was Spain's first title of this kind, and it would have to wait a long time for the next one.

1968: ITALY CONQUERS EUROPE

Euro 1968 took place in Italy, with three cities hosting the games: Florence, Rome, and Naples. Like the previous tournaments, there were only four teams: Italy, the Soviet Union, Yugoslavia, and England. In Italy's first game against the Soviet Union... well, how does one explain this? The game ended in a 0-0 draw and Italy eventually won by a coin toss. That's right. You heard it here. A *coin toss*. A coin toss won the game. Okay. You might ask, "How is that possible?" Only in Italy. (Was that coin regulation?) Moving on. That was one semi-final. In the other semi-final, you had Yugoslavia versus England. In that game, Yugoslavia came out on top and met Italy—the gracious hosts— in the final. The championship took place on June 8, 1968, in the legendary Stadio Olimpico, in Rome, which turned out to be the *first game*. Approximately 68,000 people filled the stands. It was a 1-1 draw. To decide the victor, another game was played a few days later on June 10, 1968. For this match, only around 32,000 showed up. Perhaps the sentiment was 'Egh, another coin toss? Another delayed game? We'll read about it in the paper.' The Italians eventually won 2-0 and became champions of Europe. It was a great achievement for Italy; this trophy added to the list of major championships alongside two World Cup titles from 1934 and 1938. To date, it would be the last European title for Italy.

1972: WEST GERMANY IS TOO GOOD

Euro 1972 represented a great year for West Germany. The tournament was held in Belgium, a small neighbor geographically which allowed for easy access to the three cities that hosted: (north to south) Antwerp, Brussels, and Liege. The semi-finals kicked off with West Germany taking on Belgium in one, and Hungary against the Soviet Union in the other. Thanks to Gerd Müller, the star forward that got both goals, the West Germans defeated the hosts 2-1 for a place in the final against the mighty Soviet Union who had gotten by Hungary with a 1-0 victory.

West Germany was not to be stopped as it cruised to a 3-0 championship-winning victory over the Soviets with two goals from the magnificent Gerd Müller, who spent the majority of his career with Bayern Munich, and one from Herbert Wimmer, a midfielder from Borussia Monchengladbach. This was a fine era in West German football. It was a team that also featured Paul Breitner, a relentless midfielder and defender that added a great deal of depth to the outside attack, and, Franz Beckenbauer, the graceful defender that moved like a "Queen on the chessboard" throughout the field, controlling the game with smart passing and decisive movement forward. This Euro 1972 championship served as a springboard for the 1974 World Cup, which West Germany would win as well.

1976: CZECHOSLOVAKIA TAKES THE TITLE

Still following the same format, Euro 1976 featured Czechoslovakia, the Netherlands, Yugoslavia, and West Germany. Yugoslavia hosted, yet from the get-go, things started going Czechoslovakia's way. In its first game against the Netherlands, Czechoslovakia won 3-1 and found itself in the championship game with West Germany, the defending champs. A few crucial goals were scored as the game ended in a 2-2 tie. Czechoslovakia took home the trophy by way of penalty-kicks.

1980: WEST GERMANY WINS

For UEFA Euro 1980, Italy hosted and games were played in fabulous Turin, amazing Milan, romantic Rome, and nifty Naples. The tournament finally increased in the number of teams. There were two groups. Group 1 had West Germany, Czechoslovakia, Netherlands, and Greece. Group 2 consisted of Belgium, Italy, England, and Spain.

In Group 1, West Germany came out on top, with Czechoslovakia in second. In Group 2, Belgium came out on top, with Italy in second. As a result, the winners of each group moved into the final. Therefore, it was West Germany versus Belgium, and West Germany won by a score of 2-1, with goals from Horst Hrubesch (who recently coached the women's national team of Germany).

1984: FRANCE, ANYONE?

By 1984, French soccer was on the rise thanks to one man: Michel Platini. Platini, arguably France's greatest player of all time, was an elegant passing savant with uncanny skill and vision, combined with a will to score goals with power shots, touch shots, and, perhaps most of all, a deft ability to finish free-kicks with remarkable accuracy. Platini was, without a doubt, France's leader and star player. He is considered one of soccer's all-time greats as well. As for his time as UEFA's president, that's another story. During his prime in 1984, he wasn't alone. Alongside the French maestro were phenomenal talents that included Giresse (a smart, technically sound, elegant passer), Tigana (a quick, untouchable, brilliant dribbler), and Rochteau (a formidable scoring threat).

This group had done phenomenally well in the 1982 World Cup whereby France reached the semi-finals and lost in an epic overtime, penalty-shootout to West Germany. There was high drama, with remarkable goals and a memorable injury to a French player caused by a ruthless collision with the aggressive German keeper, Harald Schumacher; as a result, the French player was taken off on a stretcher.

France had gotten so close to World Cup glory but it wasn't meant to be. Two years down the road, it was seasoned and ready for the big-time. The Euro Cup was a prime opportunity to assert its dominance in Europe. France had an added advantage of hosting Euro 1984; the games were held in Lens, Paris, Strasbourg, Nantes, Lyon, Saint-Etienne, and Marseille. Group 1 consisted of France, Denmark, Belgium, and Yugoslavia. Group 2 was made up of Spain, Portugal, West Germany, and Romania.

In Group 1, France got off to a good start and was off and running, led by Platini who eventually scored nine goals. In its first game, the French snuck around Denmark 1-0 with a goal from Platini. Then France danced past Belgium 5-0 with a hat-trick from Platini. As for the next game, if you can believe it, Platini—who often wore his shirt untucked—showed up again with another hat-trick against Yugoslavia in a 3-2 win. Platini's skill was on full display. Who could stop the French? At this point, it was looking like France was the team to beat. Momentum was on its side. The crowd was on its side. Could this be the year? Could France win its first major trophy? France and Denmark advanced out of Group 1.

Though in Group 2, Spain had a party of its own going on…a less exciting party, but a celebration nonetheless—one that eventually advanced it from the group. Spain, France's neighbor and historical friend and foe, started out the tournament with a 1-1 tie against Romania. This was followed up by another 1-1 tie against Portugal, with a goal from Santillana (a forward that played many years with Real Madrid). Finally, in its last group match, Spain got a 1-0 win over West Germany with a goal from Antonio Maceda.

Next up were the semi-finals. Spain would go onto defeat Denmark in a penalty shootout. Meanwhile, France stepped past Portugal 3-2 with one goal contributed from Platini.

The stage was set for a showdown between France and Spain. In the final, which was held in Paris, Platini delivered yet again with a goal that helped France defeat Spain 2-0. France, finally, was on top of the world by way of European greatness.

1988: THE REMARKABLE DUTCH

UEFA Euro 1988 was a special tournament. West Germany played host. There was excitement in the air from the get-go. In Group 1, you had West Germany, Italy, Spain, and Denmark. In Group 2, there was the Soviet Union, Netherlands, Ireland, and England.

In Group 1, the dazzling Danes, who had showed so much promise in the 1986 World Cup, ended up placing last. Spain ended up getting a win, with two losses. West Germany and Italy led the group and advanced to the semi-finals. For West Germany, Lothar Matthäus (a two-way talent, the general in the middle), Rudi Völler (an intuitive goal-scorer), and Jürgen

Klinsmann (a free-flowing forward with great instincts) were featured players. Italy rested its hopes in the hands of Franco Baresi (a brilliant central defender that orchestrated the possession-end of the game like a symphony conductor), Roberto Donadoni (an outstanding winger with elusive dribbling ability), and Gianluca Vialli (a marvelous scoring threat), with the popular Walter Zenga in goal.

Meanwhile, in Group 2, there was a storm brewing: A Dutch storm by the name of Ruud Gullit, Frank Rijkaard, Ronald Koeman, and Marco van Basten. Rinus Michels—the old master with experience from Ajax and Barcelona—led the squad as coach, with a glimmer in his eye and thoughts abound of taking the tournament by surprise. The first group game for the Dutch ended in a 1-0 loss at the hands of the Soviets. Though in game number two, the Dutch unleashed a flurry of goals against England, led by Bryan Robson, for a 3-1 victory. Marco van Basten was the star, with a hat-trick—a sign of things to come. It was a much-needed win for the Dutch as the team took this momentum into its final game against Ireland, and walked away with a narrow 1-0 win.

As a result, Ireland and England were left behind as Netherlands and the Soviet Union marched into the semi-finals.

Everybody was anticipating the colossal showdown—which it was—between West Germany and Netherlands. Rinus Michels on one bench and Franz Beckenbauer on the other. Excitement was sparkling in the air. All eyes were on this game. Matthäus got West Germany on the board first with a penalty kick that barely got through the hands of the Dutch keeper. Only one word can describe his reaction after scoring: relief. Towards the end of the game, following a questionable foul against van Basten in the German box, a penalty kick was awarded and the game rested on one kick by Koeman. With all of the pressure in the world on one moment, he delivered calmly and tied the game at 1-1. It looked like extra time but before you knew it, a pass sent into the box for van Basten ended in a late-game goal that sent Netherlands past the talented Germans and into the final.

In the other semi-final, the Soviets got past a formidable Italian side by a score of 2-0 with goals from Hennadiy Lytovchenko and Oleh Protasov.

The final saw two goals from Netherlands that sealed the deal; the first came from Gullit and the second was a miraculous first-time volley taken from a cross that van Basten somehow guided into the opposite corner of the goal. The latter was a once-in-a-lifetime goal, yet he made it look so normal. The Dutch were European champions, and deserving ones at that.

1992: THE DANES SHOW UP BIG TIME

Who could have anticipated what happened in Euro 1992? The answer would be very few, if any.

Sweden, the great Scandinavian country of the north, hosted. Group 1 consisted of Sweden, Denmark, France, and England. Sweden and Denmark escaped. Group 2 had Netherlands, Germany, Scotland, and CIS. Netherlands and Germany got through. In the semi-finals, Denmark defeated Netherlands in a penalty-kick shootout, and Germany slid past Sweden by a score of 3-2.

In the final, Denmark, the unexpected champions, swept the floor with Germany. It was big news around the world. In the US—which, in 1992, was a place that had little patience for soccer—*The New York Times* covered the story: "Denmark, invited here only after Yugoslavia was banned from international competition, captured its first major soccer championship by beating Germany, 2-0, tonight in the final of the European championship."[14]

Who would've thought? The Danes came out on top, shocking the world in the process. Keep in mind, Denmark had always produced quality players such as Preben Elkjaer, Michael Laudrup, and Jesper Olsen, to name a few, but its biggest achievement—in recent years leading up to the 1992 Euro—was probably the run it had in the 1986 World Cup, which sparkled in the group phase but fizzled out quickly in the Round of 16 to Spain by a score of 5-1 (not exactly taking the world by storm). For Denmark, winning the 1992 Euro was its biggest accomplishment to date.

Will Denmark do it again any time soon? It is possible but unlikely. Is it highly unlikely? No, not at all, but it's definitely unlikely. It would need a unique generation of players to topple the best Europe has to offer, and such a group is currently unavailable.

1996: THE GERMANS WIN AGAIN

UEFA Euro 1996 was hosted by England, the inventors of the game. Games were held in Newcastle, Leeds, Liverpool, Manchester, Sheffield, Nottingham, Birmingham, and London.

England hadn't had much luck in past Euro Cups and this wasn't about to change.

The number of teams increased this time around which was a nice change. Say what you will, the addition of more teams is here to stay. It could be successfully argued that by opening up the tournament to more teams, you are simply watering down the competition. People that espouse this line of thought might sarcastically say, "Hell, let's just let everyone in!" Though, it could also argued that more teams ultimately provide a lot more entertainment value. Wherever you might land, the end result is clear: This tournament represented the addition of more teams and (as things currently stand) there's no turning back. More teams equal more action for fans, and more money across the board for the organizers.

Group A had England, Netherlands, Scotland, and Switzerland. Group B had France, Spain, Bulgaria, and Romania. Group C consisted of Germany, Czech Republic, Italy, and Russia. Group D had Portugal, Croatia, Denmark, and Turkey.

On route to the final, Germany, the eventual champions, went through Croatia in the quarter-finals by a score of 2-1 (with goals from Jürgen Klinsmann and Matthias Sammer). In the semi-finals, the Germans stepped past England (which ended dramatically in penalty kicks; fortunately, for Germany, one English player, Gareth Southgate, missed). In the championship, Oliver Bierhoff led the way for Germany with both goals, ending in a 2-1 victory over the Czech Republic.

2000: THE ELEGANT FRENCH

UEFA Euro 2000, co-hosted by Belgium and Netherlands, was a sparkling tournament for France.

Cities that hosted in Belgium included Bruges, Brussels, Liege, and Charleroi, while in the Netherlands, the cities were Amsterdam, Rotterdam, Arnhem, and Eindhoven.

Group A had Portugal, Romania, England, and Germany. Group B had Italy, Turkey, Belgium, and Sweden. Group C consisted of Spain, FR Yugoslavia, Norway, and Slovenia. Group D had Netherlands, France, Czech Republic, and Denmark.

Group A was very interesting as England had issues with the tournament, as usual. It just was not meant to be for England, the inventors of the game. The English had won the 1966 World Cup, yet when the Euro came around, things were just not lining up for the Three Lions. UEFA Euro 2000 was yet another example. However, there was a little room to breathe for English fans as Germany didn't do too well either. The Germans, who were the reigning Euro Cup champs from 1996, finished last in the group, with England just ahead. Coming in second was Romania, with Portugal taking first. Was this result surprising? Yes, quite a bit. Let's put it this way. If you had a small group of people in a bar discussing who would escape the group and one of them blurted out, "Romania, of course!" that person would likely be from Romania. Not that Romania had a bad team, in fact, the Romanian World Cup squad of 1990 was amazingly good (thus establishing a precedent). But for Romania and Portugal to escape the group while England and Germany were left behind was indeed unexpected (no shocker there).

The Italians, who placed first in Group B, fielded a good team in 2000, with Francesco Totti, Filippo Inzaghi, Demetrio Albertini, Paolo Maldini, and Fabio Cannavaro leading the way. The coach dabbled with the lineup a little bit, but, this was essentially the core group that Italy was leaning on; it was a damn good one at that. Italy was excited about its prospects. Things were looking very good.

In Group C, Spain was off and running. Though it escaped a group that wasn't super-talented. In fact, if you were Spain, and the competition consisted of FR Yugoslavia, Norway, and Slovenia…say no more. That's a dream come true for Spain. FR Yugoslavia represented the toughest challenge. And say what you will about Norway and Slovenia, but, after all, it is Norway and Slovenia—two sides that represented very little threat to Spain. As to which of the two represented more of a threat to Spain, you could have probably flipped a coin.

Group D, on the other hand, had a crowded field of talent. While Denmark finished last, it was still Denmark—a good side on any day. Czech Republic, no slouch, finished in third. France— the defending World Cup champs—came in second while the Netherlands—the best nation, alongside Spain, to never win a World Cup—took first. This was arguably the toughest group of the tournament, rightly so.

Destiny was shaping up for Italy and France to meet in the final. France was stacked, with Marcel Desailly leading things on defense, not to mention the leadership of Didier Deschamps, with the sparkling play of Zidane and Henry. France first hopped past Spain in the quarter-finals, followed by Portugal in the semis.

On the other side of things, Italy got past Romania in the quarters, and then worked its way around the always-talented Netherlands in the semis.

It was a perfect matchup: France vs. Italy—two great teams at the time. Italy had three World Cup titles under its belt, with one Euro trophy as well. France, on the other hand, had one World Cup title and one Euro trophy. Italy's last World Cup title was in 1982, while its last Euro trophy was from 1968. France's World Cup title, which was from 1998, was fresh and the talent was still there; its last Euro title, on the other hand, was from 1984. It was a brilliant pairing that went to extra time. In a 2-1 victory, for the title of Europe, France got the Golden Goal from David Trezeguet and the rest was history. Add another one to France's trophy case; Zidane was the guiding force and it was a phenomenal era for sure.

2004: GREECE ACCOMPLISHES THE UNTHINKABLE

UEFA Euro 2004 landed in the great Portugal, the country by the sea. Games took place in Braga, Guimaraes, Porto, Aveiro, Coimbra, Leiria, Lisbon, and Faro/Loulé.

The teams were ready. Group A had Portugal, Greece, Spain, and Russia. Group B had France, England, Croatia, and Switzerland. Group C consisted of Sweden, Denmark, Italy, and Bulgaria. Group D included Czech Republic, Netherlands, Germany, and Latvia.

In Group A, Portugal presented the young talents of one Cristiano Ronaldo. Leading the way in midfield was the experienced Luís Figo. Portugal would win its group with the help of the 12th man, home-side fans. Greece, the unexpected heroic side of 2004, was led by Theodoros Zagorakis. In a bit of a surprise, Greece placed second in the group ahead of Spain and Russia.

As for Group B, Croatia and Switzerland predictably fell short of qualifying for the elimination rounds while France and England advanced.

In Group C, Italy and Bulgaria left disappointed as Sweden and Denmark marched forward.

There was a surprise in Group D as Germany (one of the top teams) exited early, alongside Latvia (who had low expectations). The winner of the group turned out to be Czech Republic (somewhat of a shocker), with Netherlands coming in second.

If Denmark winning in the Euro in 1992 was a surprise, then Greece winning it in 2004 was like the earth turning on its axis for 25 minutes, then freezing into a massive Ice Age for ten minutes causing everyone, everywhere, to wonder what had just happened. Well, in short, Greece, a massive underdog, just won the Euro. That is what happened. No one expected it. Not even Greece, quite frankly.

Outside of group play, Greece had a tremendous challenge. In the quarter-finals, it first had to get by France, the defending champs. And, after a concentrated effort on defense, it found a moment. Peter Berlin, writing for *The New York Times*, explained: "Zagorakis escaped Lizarazu on the right and had time to aim his ball for the head of Angelos Charisteas, who drove his close-range header past Barthez."[15] The result was a 1-0 victory, a much-needed 1-0 victory.

Then, to the joy of Greeks everywhere, the unexpected wonder got past Czech Republic by a familiar elimination-round score of 1-0 in the semis.

Perhaps, whether it is the ancient times or today, legends are made when the task at hand is one that seems larger than life itself. Achilles, and the Greek forces, conquered Hector and the unconquerable walls of Troy. An epic war occurred and history was made. Thousands of years later, Greece, in its humble arrogance, was taking on the best of Europe in 2004. Theodoros Zagorakis was a key figure on Greece's quest for greatness. His leadership was crucial for success. Someday, many generations from now, his myth will live on, alongside that of stories from the ancient times.

As for the final, the Greeks had a stern test ahead. Portugal, the home side, was in its way. Portugal was a talented group that featured Figo and C. Ronaldo; with these two players (alone) standing in the way, many coaches would suffer sleepless nights. Though, in true Greek fashion (to this point in the elimination rounds, anyway), a 1-0 victory sealed the deal. In doing so, the victory elevated Greece to the highest point in European soccer, thus creating an eternal chapter in the history books for the ancient land of democracy, philosophy, and theater.

2008: SPAIN IS NUMBER ONE AFTER A LONG WAIT

UEFA Euro 2008 was a brilliant tournament and also a beginning of something special for Spain.

Austria and Switzerland co-hosted. In Austria, games were held in Vienna, Salzburg, Innsbruck, and Klagenfurt. Switzerland featured the wonderful cities of Basel, Zurich, Bern, and Geneva.

It was a beautiful setting, one that some people have spent thousands of dollars to hike in. The tournament was ready to go.

Group A had Portugal, Turkey, Czech Republic, and Switzerland. Group B had Croatia, Germany, Austria, and Poland. Group C consisted of Netherlands, Italy, Romania, and France. Group D rounded things up with Spain, Russia, Sweden, and Greece.

In Group A, Portugal and Turkey escaped while Czech Republic and Switzerland did not play as well. Croatia and Germany led Group B while Austria and Poland were out. As it turned out, both host nations—Austria and Switzerland—were unable to advance past the group phase (not a big surprise, but worth noting nonetheless).

Group C definitely had a strong field of teams. Anytime you have the Netherlands, Italy, and France in a group, things are going to be highly competitive. Although, none of them won the tournament so perhaps they wore each other out. Having said that, the Netherlands and Italy advanced, while Romania and France were eliminated.

In Group D, Spain started out by cruising to a 4-1 victory over Russia with a big game from David Villa. Backing up Villa were Xavi, Iniesta, David Silva, Puyol, and Sergio Ramos. In its next match, Spain held back Zlatan Ibrahimović and outdid Sweden 2-1 with goals from Fernando Torres and Villa. Last up in the group for Spain was Greece. Again, the Spaniards delivered with a 2-1 win.

In the quarter-finals, Spain maneuvered past the defiant Italians in a penalty-kick shootout. In the semis, Spain encountered Russia, which ended up being a 3-0 win (no surprise there). As for the final, Spain had to get through Germany, who featured Bastian Schweinsteiger, Michael Ballack, Lukas Podolski, and Miroslav Klose, a potent attack to say the least. It was shaping up to be a perfect opportunity for Spain. *The New York Times* printed, "The Spaniards, who have long been considered one of soccer's biggest underachievers, will play old rival Germany for the championship on Sunday."[16] Indeed Spain was known as a country that had quality but failed to conquer big tournaments. (With the exception of Euro 1964, Spain's one glorious achievement was beginning to come across as a long-lost, distant memory, which it would seem, had either been forgotten or overlooked by most fans around the world.) If Spain were to change its perception, as an underachiever, it would need to pull everything together for this game. Games often come down to a simple moment, one defiant moment to change the course of history. With a burst of acceleration from Torres, along with a possible foul committed against Philipp Lahm, the lone goal, which ended up being the decider, was scored. And so it was. Spain found itself on top of Europe.

This was the second Euro title for Spain. On an individual level, the leading goal-scorer was David Villa. The UEFA Player of the Tournament went to Xavi. But, individual awards aside, it was the start of something monumental for Spain. Following 2008, it would go onto win the 2010 World Cup, and the 2012 Euro, a triple; three in a row; this had never been done before by any other European side. Now, it could be said that Brazil accomplished the same thing by winning the 2002 World Cup, the 2004 Copa America, and, last but not least, the 2007 Copa America, all in a row. However, it could be easily argued that the Copa America is not as competitive as the UEFA Euro. There just are not enough viable teams in South America. Hence, Spain's accomplishment is much more impressive. As such, Euro 2008 was special as it was the first in this amazing run for Spain, a team (with a few different players that came and went) that will live eternally as one of the greatest to ever play.

2012: SPAIN DOES IT AGAIN!

UEFA Euro 2012 was co-hosted by Poland and Ukraine. Cities in Poland that hosted were Gdansk, Poznan, Warsaw, and Wroclaw. In Ukraine, the games were played in Kiev, Lviv, Kharkiv, and Donetsk.

Group A had Czech Republic, Greece, Russia, and Poland. Group B had Germany, Portugal, Denmark, and Netherlands. Group C consisted of Spain, Italy, Croatia, and Republic of Ireland. Group D rounded things off with England, France, Ukraine, and Sweden.

Group A, probably the least exciting of the groups, saw Czech Republic and Greece go through while Russia and Poland failed to advance.

Group B, a violently competitive group, one that was worth its weight in gold, saw Germany and Portugal advance while Denmark and Netherlands were left behind. This was probably the toughest group in the tournament.

Group C was interesting and had the capability to make you stop and think. While Spain and Italy moved on, Croatia and Republic of Ireland made things interesting. Spain, a team on a path with destiny, started out by tying Italy 1-1, with a goal from Cesc Fàbregas. Then Spain dropped Ireland off at the cleaners with a 4-0 trouncing, no surprise there. Croatia offered the Spaniards a stiffer challenge, though Spain managed to get by with a 1-0 victory thanks to a goal from Jesús Navas, the speedy winger.

Meanwhile, in the distant land of Group D, England and France finished atop the standings while Ukraine and Sweden had to say goodbye.

Spain was all the rave, with incredible passing combinations linking up all around the field. Spain's key players, Xavi and Iniesta, led the way. These two were the central pieces that made everything click. There was plenty of help from Pique, Sergio Ramos, and David Silva, among others. The notorious style of tiki-taka (a short-passing nightmare for opponents) was moving full-steam ahead. No one could stop it. In fact, the TV show *Ancient Aliens* proposed that one way to travel vast distances in space would be to utilize self-replicating robots that establish outposts along the way for future travelers to use; in this process, the pre-programed robots would self-replicate and reduplicate certain things for survival. Perhaps Spain's style of play was coming across as robots reduplicating passes, over and over again. It would seem that wherever the Spaniards went on the field, a barrage of short-passing combinations followed with a frequency that seemed to follow a higher mathematical code. Something…quite robotic. Robotic and beautiful. It was proving effective as the Spanish were rolling along with authority. If Spain was great in 2008, this was Spain 3.0.

The quarter-finals were up next and the Spanish took on France. Thanks to Xabi Alonso, who scored twice, Spain advanced to the semis whereby it confronted an eager Portuguese side, led by Cristiano Ronaldo and Nani. After a 0-0 tie, Spain won in a penalty shootout—a big relief for the Spanish as any shootout can be unpredictable and go either way. The final was all set for a showdown between Spain and Italy. As it turned out, Italy was no match for the dominant Spanish. In fact, Spain, who was playing brilliant possession-oriented soccer, coasted to a 4-0 win and racked up its third Euro title in total. Of course, the 2012 title represented the second in a row as Spain had won in 2008. Not to mention, it had just won the 2010 World Cup in South Africa. Three major titles in a row. Steven Goff, writing for *The Washington Post*, summed up what most everyone was thinking, "With a resounding victory over Italy on Sunday, Spain submitted a formidable claim to be recognized as one of the greatest national teams in soccer history."[17] The Golden Generation, as this Spanish side came to be known, was riding high. It was an accomplishment for the ages, one that may never be equaled.

2016: PORTUGAL SHOCKS THE WORLD

For UEFA Euro 2016, there was a little pressure for France, the hosts. According to *The New York Times*, "In simple sporting terms, the 2016 European Championship starting Friday has to live up to the legacy of 1984, when France last hosted and won the Euro, with Michel Platini, the team's most inspirational player and leader, as the star."[18] A few teams favored going into the 2016 tournament were Germany and Spain. France was among those in consideration. However, Real Madrid star Karim Benzema, one of France's best forwards, was left off the team. Go figure. It's France. What can you say? Antoine Griezmann was expected to step up and lead the way for the French. As such, France was gearing up and ready to go. The excitement was palpable.

French cities that hosted games were Villeneuve-d'Ascq, Lens, Saint-Denis, Paris, Décines-Charpieu, Saint-Etienne, Bordeaux, Nice, Toulouse, and Marseille.

Group A featured France, Switzerland, Albania, and Romania. Group B had Wales, England, Slovakia, and Russia. Group C consisted of Germany, Poland, Northern Ireland, and Ukraine. Group D had Croatia, Spain, Turkey, and Czech Republic. Group E had Italy, Belgium, Republic of Ireland, and Sweden. Group F rounded things off with Hungary, Iceland, Portugal, and Austria. As expected, France, the hosts, advanced out of Group A.

In Group B, Wales—led by Gareth Bale of Real Madrid— wound up taking first, while England finished in respectable second place. In his book, *The Shadow War: Inside Russia's and China's Secret Operations to Defeat America*, Jim Sciutto reflects on Russia and China having weapons in space, including lasers, which orbit around earth, waiting, potentially, to strike. Russia did not have quite the arsenal for the soccer pitch this time around. In disappointing fashion, Russia finished last, behind lesser known Slovakia.

As for Group C, Germany predictably took first place. In second was Poland, followed by Northern Ireland, and last but not least, was Ukraine. In Group D, Croatia took first, while Spain ended up second. Turkey and Czech Republic (shocker) left early. Group E saw Italy, Belgium and Republic of Ireland advance, while Sweden went home early. Finally, in Group F, Hungary,

Iceland, and Portugal advanced. Austria did not. In fact, the Portuguese barely got through after tying each game. The third place teams that moved ahead were Slovakia, Republic of Ireland, Portugal, and Northern Ireland.

Portugal met Croatia in the Round of 16 and snuck by with a 1-0 win. Moving past Poland in the quarter-finals required the help of a penalty-kick shootout which Portugal aced. A 2-0 win in the semis pushed Portugal past Wales.

Portugal had Ronaldo and Nani. Though it wasn't in the same class as Germany and France, it was a solid squad. Few were expecting what would eventually happen.

Elsewhere, a new story was building from an unlikely source.

Iceland made huge waves this tournament. Who would have thought? Yes, somehow Iceland was playing well and escaped the group stage. As a small island-nation that only recently put itself on the world map of soccer, Iceland confronted the mighty English in the Round of 16, a game surely to be won by the Three Lions. Things, however, went Iceland's way. As *CNN* reported, "Iceland pulled off one of the most astonishing results in the history of European football on Monday, knocking England out of the Euro 2016 finals."[19] England was devastated and embarrassed. Iceland, on the other hand, was riding high. The Icelandic fans were methodically chanting and clapping, and the earth seemed to move. Iceland's team had a unique vibe about it. The players seemed to enjoy themselves, showing good team chemistry. To step onto the grand stage of the Euro with such confidence, without much history to draw on, was remarkable. In lieu of not winning the tournament, Iceland made a huge impression.

In the Round of 16, France predictably got past Ireland. Then the French stepped around a possible upset-disaster in the quarter-finals by ending the run of Iceland. In the semis, France outdid the talented Germans by a score of 2-0.

The championship was all set: France vs. Portugal. It seemed like France was destined to add another trophy to its case. Sure, Portugal had Cristiano Ronaldo and Nani, but France had a full deck of cards (one could argue four Queens) and was flowing in its rhythm. Griezmann was playing well; his supporting cast was revving on all cylinders. Certainly, France was the favorite. However, Portugal had other ideas and stood its ground. In extra time, Portugal got the goal it needed from Eder to secure a win. And so it was: Portugal did it. Portugal finally won a major tournament. Despite the fantastic accomplishment, there was plenty of doubt surrounding Portugal's victory. *Fox News* covered the story and Ryan Rosenblatt wrote, "Portugal wouldn't have even made the knockout stages if it wasn't for the expanded 24-team format. They finished third in their group, having not won a single match, and at any other Euros would have gone home then. But thanks to the new format, third place teams advanced and they went through."[20] Very true. Even with that said, in a peculiar way, Portugal was very deserving of the title. Following the championship match, what many people overlooked was the fact that Portugal was the underdog, playing against a phenomenal—and superior—French side, in France, in front of a home crowd and millions of fans around the world expecting a win from France. However, in defiant fashion, Portugal held on and delivered a 1-0 victory even after Cristiano Ronaldo—its star and one of the best to ever play—left the game with an injury. Reporting for *CNN*, James Masters wrote, "When he left the action after 25 minutes it was assumed that Portugal's hopes followed too."[21] However, Portugal stood its ground and when Ronaldo resided to the bench, the team arguably played better, instead of having the offense consciously or unconsciously go through him. They stepped up and made it work, surprising many in the process. It was an interesting result, to say the least. Very few people, if any, expected Portugal to win it all.

And there lies the paradox of UEFA Euro 2016. Was Portugal the best team that year? No. Did Portugal deserve the title? In a way, yes. But doubters also have a valid point. Even so, it was the first major title for Portugal and its fans are surely less concerned with doubters and more content with the fact that, for once, Portugal became number one.

UEFA EURO 2020 PREDICTIONS

INTRODUCTION TO PREDICTIONS

My following stance on predictions, laid out in *The Women's World Cup 2019 Book* and *European Soccer Leagues 2019*, is worth reiterating. Predictions are always a tricky business. Sometimes it's obvious which team will win. Other times, it is a total mystery. Though, when it comes to soccer, predictions can be very interesting. As someone who has made many successful soccer predictions, I can speak to this following point with absolute conviction: Sometimes everything goes completely wrong. It happens. That is just the world of predictions. The underdog wins, and the score is way off, and you have no idea how it happened. Or the prediction was exactly right. It should go without saying, but it is worth saying nonetheless: Soccer predictions are unpredictable. Though, sometimes it is not as hard as it looks. And I would like to think that I am pretty good. When it is right, which I must say is more often than not, the predictions usually have a lot to do with the following criteria: star power, recent team history, overall team history, current injuries, coaches, uniforms, the type of training structure each nation has, and, not to mention, a good old-fashioned hunch.

Star power has a lot to do with accurate predictions. Who are the leaders of the team? What do they offer? Are the stars offensive or defensive players? How old are they? Stars play a huge role in the outcomes of games and the overall result of tournaments. So to say stars play an important role in determining the outcome of a prediction is a complete understatement. For instance, if Ruud Gullit is on a particular team…bet on that team. Then, if somehow Marco van Basten is on that very same team…bet on that team. If you really want to go further, and you realize that not only are Ruud Gullit and Marco van Basten on the same team, but there is also someone named Frank Rijkaard (and the year happens to be 1988), then what are you waiting for? Go and put your money on that team! Every time!

Recent team history is very important for obvious reasons and should not be overlooked. If a team is on a roll, then it is usually a good thing, and you want to take that into consideration for predictions. However, you have to watch closely because sometimes a team might be on a roll after royally defeating less talented teams in friendlies, for example. Be cautious and also realize that good teams going through slumps might be a good thing for that particular team in question. Sometimes good teams need a slump to get jumpstarted back in the right direction. Of course, in this type of scenario, you would have to consider other factors, which include whether or not the team in a slump has legitimate star players, the age of the players, the style of play the team uses, and so on.

Overall team history is very important. It's also a little mysterious, and, maybe for this reason I like it the best. You see, even though you might be looking at two completely different teams, with completely different players, and a 20-year gap might even be in between the teams in question, they still get similar results. It is like an invisible force that transcends time. Though, it should be pointed out, that it's not as mysterious as it may originally seem. What happens is, over time the veterans from an older team end up coaching and pass on their ideas of how the game should be played, and, hence, a certain style is established. Not to mention, the youth academies—which receive the same structured coaching—play a huge role in developing players, and, hence, a style. These youth academies eventually should (in theory) transcend to the national team. This is an example of how teams from different eras can play alike and get similar results. There is also a psychological element involved. There is an edge that players get just from putting on a certain uniform. Take Italy, for example. Since Italy has already won past World Cups, along with one Euro, this carries with it a certain confidence and swagger (despite Italy enduring a recent slump). In other words, when new players are called up to the Italian national team, these players know that they are the best of the best. There is no doubt in their minds. They are representing a national team that has multiple championships. There is a history there. So when they put on the coveted Italian jersey, they are endowed with a certain confidence over other teams. A swagger. Vice versa, when a player from a less talented national team, like Bulgaria, puts on their respected jersey, it should indeed be a special moment, and a proud one at that, but there is not the same confidence that goes along with it. This is partially why overall team histories matter when making predictions.

Current injuries—and past injuries, for that matter—play a role in how a team performs. This is a pretty common-sense factor worth considering, but it's not always accurate. Injuries matter, but sometimes players can overcome them.

Coaches obviously have a lot to do with how well a team plays. If we are at a tournament, any tournament, and you tell me Carlo Ancelotti is coaching one of the teams, I am immediately going to assume that his team will likely do very well in the tournament in question. It is that simple. I know he recruits well. On top of that, I know his approach to the game. The same goes for Pep Guardiola. Both coaches have very high soccer IQs, along with a vast amount of experience, and coaching matters. Take Coach Joachim Löw of Germany. He is another good example of a coach that you would want to bet on. He falls in line with any great coach from around the world in that his team will likely come out on top.

Uniforms. First of all, fashion matters in sports. Hence, uniforms matter. We will return to this momentarily. Secondly, let me just say this: I'm a fashion guy. I can't help it. I didn't choose to be one. I just am. Basically, my mom took me shopping all the time growing up, and she is originally from LA, a fashion leader in the world, and she definitely knows how to put outfits together, so I know a little something about the field. (Ann Taylor—which was very popular in the 80s—is a store I spent far too much time in; I'll leave it at that.) Back to sports. Uniforms matter in sports. In essence, players will perform based on how they feel, and how they feel has a lot to do with what they are wearing. Are you telling me that if a team wore tuxedos during a game, they would perform normally? Okay, case closed. Fashion does matter. In addition to this, there is scientific research showing that what people wear really does influence how they view themselves, think of themselves, and act in general. So yes, fashion does impact human behavior, and the way that players perform in sports.

I will use an example from the Men's World Cup in 2018. Germany had its traditional look of white-black-white (a white shirt, black shorts, white socks). From the outset, this is fine. Don't get me wrong, a basic, simple uniform is often the best thing to trigger the best possible performance out of players. Traditionally, Germany has had a nice, simple uniform. However, Adidas was the sponsor for Germany in 2018, and the particular design that Adidas provided for many, if not all, of its teams had three stripes on the shoulders of the uniforms. In

Germany's case, it was three black stripes on the shoulders of a white uniform which really stood out, in a non-flowing way. The fashion sense of this choice was just off, there is no other way to put it. It is hard to explain but it just was not working. (From the beginning, I had a feeling that it was going to negatively affect the way the players played. It was a feeling of trepidation, if you will. And we are talking about one simple design flaw, something that would drive Tim Gunn crazy.) From the get-go, Germany was not playing right. And, lo and behold, things didn't go well for the Germans. In fact, Germany, the defending champs, could not even get out of its group. And on top of that, its play was less than inspiring, just like its uniforms.

Now, did Germany's bad result have something to do with the uniforms? Yes, I strongly believe it did, but how much is debatable. So in essence, uniforms matter, and if something is out of sync with a particular design, it might influence the way a team plays.

The type of training structure each national team has is very important. By "training structure," I am referring to a nation's overall soccer infrastructure. So you have to ask yourself: What sort of training structure does each nation have? And by nation, I literally mean all levels of soccer within a particular nation. I am focusing on a nation's overall training structure because this determines how youth players are trained growing up, which also eventually determines how they will play at the top national team level. Something that would also be important is a nation's club structure. La Masia, of Barcelona, is a prime example; it has provided structure for its players, a road map if you will, that has set Barcelona apart from other La Liga sides. It trains youth players for Barcelona and some of these players might eventually represent the Spanish national team. Therefore, a club's overall soccer infrastructure (i.e., its training structure) is a strong indicator of how a particular club will perform, hence there is spillover to the national team. Hence, La Masia plays an important role in the training of potential national team players. So therefore, Spain benefits from highly structured successful clubs like Barcelona and Real Madrid, and, as a result, Spain has an edge over other national teams. In this regard, countries similar to Spain will likely have strong national teams.

Lastly, let's not forget a good old-fashioned hunch. In other words, common sense. Sometimes you just have a feeling and have to go with it.

With all these factors combined, you have the reasoning behind the predictions. All in all, predictions should be a lot of fun while they also provide useful information for fans about the players and teams.

Now let's get into the predictions, shall we?

UEFA EURO 2020 PREDICTIONS

Where do we start? Will Portugal repeat as champions? Absolutely not. UEFA Euro 2016 was phenomenal for Ronaldo, Nani, and company, but this time around, Portugal will not win the whole thing. In fact, it would not be surprising if Portugal exited in the group stage. Now, will Portugal be competitive? Yes, but I would not count on the Portuguese doing very much this tournament, and it might take 36 years minimum before it wins the Euro again.

Germany will walk away as champions. You can count on that. There is a slight possibility that things won't work out for the Germans. But, by and large, Germany is ready for a strong showing. After a weak 2018 World Cup, and a less than spectacular semi-final showing in the 2016 Euro against France (a 2-0 loss), the Germans are due for a big tournament. Watch out for Germany.

France will likely do very well. The 2018 World Cup champs are soaring with confidence and this could be a great tournament for the French. In fact, in all likelihood, it will be a great tournament. But I don't see France winning the whole thing. I would not be surprised at all if France did win the whole thing, but my hunch rests with Germany. Though France is top-notch and good things will revolve around it throughout the tournament. However, will we see a classic French meltdown like in World Cups 2002 and 2010? It's very possible. You never know with France. Anything could happen. Will it take 54 years for France to win the Euro again? Probably not. But I have doubts that 2020 is France's year.

England. Where do we begin? First off, as you probably know by now, England has never won the UEFA Euro. Go figure. True to form, the English won the 1966 World Cup, what a great team that was, but there hasn't been much luck on the UEFA Euro stage. Again, go figure. It is a weird relationship that England has had with the UEFA Euro. Maybe this will be the year. It's very possible. In fact, don't be surprised at all if England manages to win the whole thing. It has a good team and is a group of guys coming off of a strong 2018 World Cup. That's important. It is a confidence boost that tells a team it belongs on the highest stage. That might just be the thing England needs right about now. However, when it's all said and done, England will likely place third overall.

Spain is too good to overlook. Spain has every reason to win this 2020 UEFA Euro—strong players, good coaching, experience, a mastery of possession. It is just a good team all around. But, where Spain might struggle is in the goal department. Will Spain get 72 shots on goal? Maybe not. That is asking a lot. However, count on Spain for a stellar tournament. It will likely make the semi-finals, but that's it. No championship this time around for Spain.

Italy has every opportunity to make this a turnaround year. It hasn't had much luck with major tournaments lately. However, if any nation can pull it together for a championship run, it is Italy. In fact, 108 years could go by and Italy will probably be a favorite to win the Euro. Will the Italians take this tournament by storm and win the whole thing? It's very possible. However, I don't see Italy doing just that in 2020. Count on an interesting show from Italy, even though it probably won't advance past the quarter-finals.

Russia. Russia will have a decent showing but will not make it past the quarter-finals. If it does, congratulations, but, in all likelihood, it probably will not get to the semi-finals.

Honduras. Wait, Honduras isn't in the tournament. I was just checking if you are paying attention. Next.

Netherlands. The Netherlands is another nation that can win the whole thing in a heartbeat. It has one Euro Cup under its belt, from 1988, and another one is looming. But I would not expect it to be in 2020. Look forward to a good performance from the Dutch but no trophies.

Belgium should have a good showing. Don't be surprised to see the Belgians in the semi-finals, and, perhaps, the final.

Croatia will have a standout tournament but win the whole thing it will not. Don't be surprised to see Luka Modrić awarded MVP of the tournament.

Switzerland almost always disappoints. No offense to Swiss people anywhere, but it's true. We're talking about its soccer team by the way, not Swiss people in general. There's always something lacking with the Swiss national team that includes creativity, a will to win, and goal-scoring. Regardless, if Switzerland wins, it usually just forces a win somehow. Therefore, I have little confidence that Switzerland will make 2020 its big year and I highly doubt the Swiss will win the tournament, much less win a game in the elimination rounds. Having said that, it wouldn't be surprising to see the Swiss get into the Round of 16. If luck is on its side (which it will most definitely need to be) it might get into the quarter-finals. But, when it's all said and done, I predict that Switzerland has a hard time getting out of its group.

Ukraine has a great chance to make a name for itself this tournament. Ukraine's big drawback might be finishing. If only Ukraine can get more points on the board. That will likely be its downfall. However, don't count Ukraine out just yet. It is a quality side that can make a run with things lining up correctly. Whether that happens is yet to be seen. Don't expect too much from Ukraine, but, at the same time, it might surprise a few people. I suspect Ukraine makes the knockout round, but it shouldn't get past the quarter-finals.

Sweden, like Hungary, will probably escape its group but that's it.

Poland should get to the quarter-finals. After that, it's a coin toss.

Austria will accomplish at least one thing this tournament: Packing its bags after failing to escape the group stage.

Turkey might make a few waves but don't expect too much. Turkey will probably escape its group but that should be it.

Dear Finland, the wonderful people of Finland: Your team has no chance of winning the 2020 UEFA Euro. Your best hope is to advance out of the group stage by tying each game and moving ahead based on point differential. I predict this won't happen. But if it does and you somehow find yourself in the Round of 16, the best option would be to hope for penalty-kicks. Then, maybe if you move on, you can use the same strategy in the quarter-finals. But, in all seriousness, Finland is not getting out of its group. So let's not even contemplate the extremely delusional scenario of the semi-finals and final, by which Finland would rely on the old penalty-kick strategy. Good luck next time.

Czech Republic will not get very far. You can count on that.

Denmark. Who said Denmark wasn't ready to repeat as champs? Anything's possible with the Danes. Watch out for a push from Denmark throughout the elimination rounds. However, Denmark will probably not emerge as champions.

Wales. Let's hear it for Wales. Keep in mind, this might be the only form of celebration Wales will see throughout the tournament. Gareth Bale is the only hope for the team, more or less. The problem with this is that he's an outside player without much support from central positions; outside players need instrumental play from central positions in order to flourish. Without help, Bale cannot be expected to carry this team very far. It's a talented side, but one that will have a hard time getting into the semi-finals.

These were fun predictions, especially for Finland.

WHAT ABOUT THE LOCATIONS?

The 2020 UEFA Euro took a unique step this time around. It focused the locations in many different places. So many, in fact, that it would take a long time to rattle them off right now. (It was already listed in the beginning of the book, by the way.) This was a vast departure from previous years. Outside of three instances when co-hosting took place—Belgium and Netherlands in 2000; Austria and Switzerland in 2008; Poland and Ukraine in 2012— the tournament has always been hosted by one nation.

For many people, one nation hosting should be the standard. It is an elite status and honor. People remember that year. Why? Because it's easy to remember one place. You associate that one place with the tournament.

For other folks, the idea of multiple nations hosting is a great way to bring the continent together in a celebration of the amazing UEFA Euro, which only takes place once every four years. It is hard to disagree with this crowd. The idea of multiple nations hosting is definitely an exciting one. It's definitely different. And it certainly brings together the European continent.

When it comes down to it, I am a fan of one nation hosting. However, if it is done every 20 years or so, I think multiple nations hosting is a good idea. It should only be done every once in a while though; for some kind of grand occasion.

Sure, the idea of spreading the tournament around to a number of nations keeps things interesting, yet, at the same time, from my point of view, it makes things a little confusing. Too many host nations. Maybe Platini should take over as UEFA President again; I doubt he would allow such a thing; then again, maybe he would—it might be an easy way to move money around.

Regardless, hopefully next time around the tournament will be in one nation. One nation is grand. It is a unique memory. It is one place, one tournament.

As for the 2020 UEFA Euro, multiple nations hosting was an exciting idea, a nice change of pace. The conversations about its success or lack thereof will be extremely interesting down the road as future tournaments are planned out.

AUTHOR'S NOTE

The UEFA Euro is just a phenomenal tournament. The UEFA Euro has become such a coveted event and keeps growing in strength each time around. As we discussed in the Introduction, the UEFA Euro and World Cup are truly the two best tournaments around. And, as some people think, the Euro is even more competitive. Perhaps that's an argument for another time. Though, one would be hard pressed to deny the pride each country brings—to each world-class stadium—is full of rich excitement that distinctly represents the unique cultures of Europe and the honor to win the whole thing is remarkable.

In his book *Before the Beginning*, Martin Rees—Astronomer Royal and former Master of Trinity College, Cambridge— wrote the following, "We don't yet know what types of particle might have existed in the earliest phases of the universe, and how many would survive."[22] However, we do know that life has steadily arrived to this point in time, unless it is all happening simultaneously like Richard Feynman suggested as a possibility. Regardless, we know that our universe has allowed for math, agriculture, law, architecture, a few other things here and there, along with sports. It could be said that sports are a true celebration of everything the universe has to offer. Without question, the sport of soccer currently represents the passion of its fans all over the world, which is why a tournament like UEFA Euro 2020 has gained so much popularity and prestige.

Each host city will certainly be lively with action. This presents an interesting dichotomy between people that enjoy a loud celebration and those that don't. As J.D. Salinger wrote about in *The Catcher in the Rye*: "New York's terrible when somebody laughs on the street very late at night. You can hear it for miles. It makes you feel so lonesome and depressed."[23] Without a doubt, it will be hard to stifle UEFA Euro 2020 celebrations. Parties will be going late into the night. Perhaps fans from losing teams won't be so happy to hear the noise. Perhaps local residents trying to catch some sleep won't be so happy to hear the noise. After all, not everyone is a fan of late-night noise. But one thing is certain: A Euro tournament brings with it noise, and a lot of it. Especially wherever England plays. (Even New York City and others around the world will have fans partying into the night.) Get used to it. Each host city that made a bid was hoping for such a thing because everyone knows that the noise and partying brings in lots of money.

In today's game, the money is huge. Brands like Nike and Adidas make certain to have a strong presence, as the eyes of the world are watching practically every move. It is a perfect chance to showcase new and existing items on such a grand stage.

Back in 1960, when the Soviet Union won the first Euro, players across the board essentially had the same kind of shoes: black. Nowadays, there are green, orange, aqua, purple, blue, white, and perhaps black. Back in the old days, players did not have much money. Today many players have more wealth than the actual organizers. There is one common thread though. Make no mistake, players from earlier eras—which may seem like a long time ago—knew there was something special about a European championship of nations, just as players of today feel the same way.

Let's cover a couple of things. Maybe you disagree with my assessment of certain players. I have one thing to say about that:

tough, get past it. Here's the thing, I think you will actually agree with most—if not all—of my player assessments. Many players described were studied and evaluated based on skill, soccer IQ, age, experience, talent level, and, perhaps, a few other reasons.

For example, Sergio Ramos was rated a 9.5. In fact, for his position he might be more valuable than that. But I feel like he was more affective as an outside back and now that he is in the middle, things are different. The fact that he is getting older also played into the rating.

The Key Players were selected prior to the official announcement of the UEFA Euro 2020 rosters. Obviously, coaches might make last-minute roster choices that differ from what the team has looked like in the months and years leading up to UEFA Euro 2020.

Key Player Stats will most likely change as time goes on. Players might play more games and score more goals. Or they won't. You never know. The Key Player Stats reflect a glimpse of what each player has contributed around the publishing of this book and it should give you a pretty good idea as to how many goals each player is capable of. Though, keep in mind, some players might be in a system that is not conducive to their style and might otherwise score more or less goals with a different team and coach. Having said that, to reiterate, the stat of games played and goals scored will likely change over time.

For future Euros down the road, this tournament will only get better with time.

Thank you for reading. A special thanks to Meyer & Meyer Sport, Cardinal Publishers Group, and Tommy Tang.

END NOTES

1   Joshua Robinson, "Ex-UEFA President Michel Platini Detained in Qatar World Cup Probe," *The Wall Street Journal*, updated June 18, 2019, accessed October 29, 2019, https://www.wsj.com/articles/ex-uefa-president-michel-platini-detained-in-qatar-world-cup-probe-11560855407

2   Chuck Culpepper, "Kylian Mbappe couldn't be stopped in the World Cup, and neither can hyperbole about his future," *The Washington Post*, published July 15, 2018, accessed September 14, 2019, https://www.washingtonpost.com/sports/kylian-mbappe-couldnt-be-stopped-in-the-world-cup-and-neither-can-hyperbole-about-his-future/2018/07/15/ef921c38-887a-11e8-8aea-86e88ae760d8_story.html

3   Leo Robson, "GOAL-ORIENTED, *How we watch soccer now.,*" *The New Yorker*, June 25, 2018.

4   Julyssa Lopez, "Germany's 30 most beautiful places," *CNN*, updated July 11, 2019, accessed October 21, 2019, https://www.cnn.com/travel/article/germany-beautiful-places/index.html

5   Ibid.

6   Jeff Scott, "8 ways to 'go Dutch,'" *CNN*, published July 12, 2017, accessed October 21, 2019, https://www.cnn.com/travel/article/netherlands-go-dutch/index.html

7   Meredith Bethune, "Best brewery tours in Belgium for beer lovers," *CNN*, updated August 8, 2017, accessed October 23, 2019, https://www.cnn.com/travel/article/belgium-best-brewery-tours/index.html

8   Ibid.

9   Tom Schad, "For Real Madrid's busy new winger Eden Hazard, FIFA 20 cover 'like a dream'," *USA TODAY*, published July 26, 2019, accessed September 21, 2019, https://www.usatoday.com/story/sports/soccer/2019/07/26/eden-hazard-fifa-20-cover-like-dream-new-real-madrid-winger/1830950001/

10 Bija Knowles, "Visiting Rome? Insiders share tips," *CNN*, updated July 18, 2018, accessed October 23, 2019, https://www.cnn.com/travel/article/insider-guide-rome/index.html

11 By Associated Press, "Mancini: Italy squad for Euro 2020 all but decided," *The Washington Post*, published October 7, 2019, accessed October 21, 2019, https://www.washingtonpost.com/sports/dcunited/mancini-italy-quad-for-euro-2020-all-but-decided/2019/10/07/964e8af6-e91a-11e9-a329-7378fbfa1b63_story.html

12 Ian Hawkey, "Visiting Barcelona? Insiders share their tips," *CNN*, updated October 29, 2015, accessed October 25, 2019, https://www.cnn.com/travel/article/insider-guide-barcelona/index.html

13 Patrick Radden Keefe, "The Bank Robber," *The New Yorker*, published May 23, 2016, accessed October 22, 2019, https://

www.newyorker.com/magazine/2016/05/30/herve-falcianis-great-swiss-bank-heist

14 *The New York Times. "SOCCER; It's Royal Copenhagen: Denmark Stuns Germany,"* published June 27, 1992, accessed May 13, 2019, https://www.nytimes.com/1992/06/27/sports/soccer-it-s-royal-copenhagen-denmark-stuns-germany.html

15 Peter Berlin, "EURO 2004: SOCCER: France dethroned by upstart Greece," *The New York Times*, published June 26, 2004, accessed May 18, 2019, https://www.nytimes.com/2004/06/26/sports/IHT-euro-2004-soccer-france-dethroned-by-upstart-greece.html

16 The Associated Press, *"Spain Dominates Russia and Advances to Final,"* *The New York Times*, published June 27, 2008, accessed May 24, 2019, https://www.nytimes.com/2008/06/27/sports/soccer/27soccer.html

17 Steven Goff, "After European Championship, Spain's place in soccer history must be kicked around," *The Washington Post*, published July 1, 2012, accessed May 23, 2019, https://www.washingtonpost.com/blogs/soccer-insider/post/after-european-championship-spains-place-in-soccer-history-must-be-kicked-around/2012/07/01/gJQAxJnzGW_blog.html?noredirect=on&utm_term=.5f3a3112ee11

18 Rob Hughes, "For France, Great Expectations On and Off Field," *The New York Times*, published June 9, 2016, accessed May 10, 2019, https://www.nytimes.com/2016/06/10/sports/soccer/for-france-great-expectations-on-and-off-field.html

19 James Masters, "Euro 2016: Iceland shocks England in historic upset to reach quarterfinals," *CNN*, updated June 28, 2016, accessed May 25, 2019, https://www.cnn.com/2016/06/27/football/euro-2016-england-iceland/index.html

20 Ryan Rosenblatt | FoxSports, "Portugal's Euro 2016 title was only possible because of the new 24-team format," *Fox News*, published July 10, 2016, last update July 11, 2016, accessed May 26, 2019, https://www.foxnews.com/sports/portugals-euro-2016-title-was-only-possible-because-of-the-new-24-team-format

21 James Masters, "Cristiano Ronaldo: Is Euro 2016 triumph his greatest achievement?" *CNN*, updated July 11, 2016, accessed August 19, 2019, https://www.cnn.com/2016/07/11/football/cristiano-ronaldo-euro-2016/index.html

22 Martin Rees, *Before the Beginning*, Helix Books, Perseus Books, Reading, Massachusetts, 1998, p. 111.

23 J.D. Salinger, *The Catcher in the Rye*, Little, Brown and Company, Boston, Massachusetts, 1991, p. 81.

CREDITS

Cover & interior design: Annika Naas

Layout: ZeroSoft

Cover photos: © dpa

Interior photos: © AdobeStock

Managing editor: Elizabeth Evans

Copyeditor: Qurratulain Zaheer